THE ART OF CYPRUS

«Nous autres, civilisations, nous savons que nous sommes mortelles»
("We civilizations, we know that we are mortal")
Paul Valéry

FORMS AND COLORS SERIES BOOKS
are published under the direction of André Held and D. W. Bloemena

TONY SPITERIS

THE ART OF CYPRUS

Translated from the French by Thomas Burton

REYNAL & COMPANY
in association with
WILLIAM MORROW & COMPANY INC.
NEW YORK

A FORMS AND COLORS SERIES BOOK

I wish to express my deep gratitude
to His Beatitude Archbishop Makarios, President of the Republic of Cyprus, who,
with rare understanding, supported and encouraged me
in writing this book.
I especially wish to thank
His Excellency Patroclos Stavrou, Under-Secretary of State to the President of the Republic of Cyprus,
for his interest and his unfailing and effective assistance.
My warm thanks are also due
to Dr. Vassos Karageorghis, Director of the Department of Antiquities of Cyprus,
for his valuable advice and for having generously placed at my disposal
all the equipment needed to photograph the objects in his museum.
Finally, I am grateful to Mr. Kyriakos Nicolaou, Mrs. Ino Michaelidou-Nicolaou,
Mrs. Angeliki Pieridou, Curators of the Nicosia Archeological Museum,
and all their colleagues who did so much to make my task easier.

Illustration on the jacket: Centaur. Polychrome décoration.
Classical era of Cyprus Vth–IVth Century B.C. Terra-cotta.
Heigth: 16 cm, length 11,2 cm. Cyprus Museum, Nicosia.

Cover: enlarged detail of the bowl, reproduced on page 26

CONTENTS

PREFACE

For a long time the archeology of Cyprus was both unknown to the world at large and neglected by the experts. Only a few amateurs of art and pilferers of the treasure-hunting variety, concerned exclusively with their own pleasure or profit, benefited from its existence. Among those in the former category, Luigi Palma di Cesnola, the United States consul on Cyprus from 1865 to 1867, is undoubtedly the best known. Taking advantage of his extended stay on the island, as well as his official position, Cesnola was able to assemble a very important collection, now one of the treasures of the Metropolitan Museum in New York.

At first, the art of Cyprus was regarded as merely a provincial and not very significant manifestation of the Middle Eastern Koine and, subsequently, of the Greek world. In the conventional view, as it was passed on to the public, Cypriot art was adequately represented by the spectacular colossal vase of *Amathus* and a few pieces of pottery and sculpture belonging to the Louvre. Happily, in the course of the last thirty years or so this false conception has been refuted by the facts.

The initial explorations were made during the last century, unfortunately in a wholly empirical manner. Nevertheless, it is to the courage and persistence of a few pioneers that we owe the present sound basis for further research, both in the study and in the field.

The first serious attempt at a systematic approach was made by Sir John Myres. In his role of editor of the catalogue of the Cesnola Collection after its sale to the Metropolitan Museum, he went to Cyprus, where his stratigraphical excavations enabled him to establish a relative chronology and thus date the objects and classify them according to type. The Swedish Cyprus Expedition (1927–1930) made discoveries of capital importance to the island's archeology, which was shown to have a distinctive character of its own.

Since then, the studies of other scholars, in particular, Professor Cl. F. A. Schaeffer and Dr. P. Dikaios, have thrown more light on certain aspects of the island's early history.

Since 1960, when Cyprus became independent, local archeology has benefited enormously from the vigorous policies of the dynamic Director of Antiquities, Dr. Vassos Karageorghis. His many publications, the exploration of numerous sites either for the Department of Antiquities of Cyprus (henceforth D.A.C.) or in collaboration with foreign missions, and the reorganization of the Department's services are just a few of his achievements.

The island is, in fact, one huge archeological site. There are nine foreign missions in the field, proof of the growing interest in the traces of Cyprus's past, the individuality of its ancient art, and the increasingly eminent position that it occupies in Mediterranean archeology.

It would be presumptuous of me to claim to have given an exhaustive account of the art of Cyprus in all its aspects over a period of six thousand years. In fact, my aim has been the more modest one of presenting a panoramic view of the artistic and cultural heritage of the island, a rare interfusion of elements contributed by both East and West.

Since the reader is unlikely to be already familiar with the esthetics of Cypriot art, particular care has been taken with the iconographic documentation. The accompanying text, while strictly respectful of the archeological facts, is easy to read and not overly technical. Indeed, I have tried to stress the artistic aspects of the finds as viewed by a modern observer. This approach, generally shunned by the scientific world, nevertheless brings out the originality and richness of Cypriot art.

The impact of any art book depends primarily on the quality of the reproductions. In sifting among the abundant material available, I have therefore given preference to objects whose esthetic merit is undeniable. This may have led to the illustrations being weighted slightly in favor of some aspects of certain periods of Cypriot art rather than others. My object has been to rouse the reader's curiosity and sharpen his vision, thus enabling him to decipher an intriguing message phrased in the mysterious language of all creation. The photographic quality of the objects illustrated has made this task enormously easier. Through the eye of the photographer, ever sensitive to composition, lighting and expressive detail, we are introduced to a world of recreated beauty.

The book is so arranged that the reader is initiated gradually into the unfamiliar world of Cypriot art. First, he is acquainted with the religious imperatives on which that world was based. This introduction is followed by an analysis of the distinctive features of the art of Cyprus and a chronological account of the various phases through which it has passed, all placed in their proper social and historical context.

The text is supplemented by a short bibliography and comparative tables that can be used to relate happenings on Cyprus with important events taking place concurrently in Greece and the Middle East.

IDOL.
8 *Neolithic I A (5800–5250 B.C.).* *Khirokitia (Larnaca).* *Stone (andesite). Height: 19 cm.* *Cyprus Museum, Nicosia.*

IDOL.   Stone (andesite). Height: 10 cm.
Neolithic I A (5800–5250 B.C.).
Khirokitia (Larnaca). Cyprus Museum, Nicosia.

IDOL.   Stone (andesite). Height: 9.6 cm.
Neolithic I A (5800–5250 B.C.).
Khirokitia (Larnaca). Cyprus Museum, Nicosia.

ART AND RELIGION

«La crainte a élevé des temples»
("Fear has raised temples") *Paul Valéry*

The esthetic sense has been in evidence since the dawn of humanity, but for long centuries artistic creation was inseparable from the omnipresent forces that controlled both man's earthly destiny and his life in the beyond. He feared these forces and struggled to subdue them; at the same time, he worshipped them to appease their wrath. It is not easy to penetrate the surrealistic and awe-filled atmosphere that man created in his beginnings or to understand his gropings after explanations for the confusion of the natural world.

Man has always been preoccupied by the disturbing phenomenon of death. The care lavished upon the preparation of a tomb proof against wild animals and the ravages of time,

BOWL WITH SPOUT.   *Stone (andesite). Height: 10 cm, width: 21.5 cm.*
Neolithic I A (5800–5250 B.C.).   *Khirokitia (Larnaca).*   *Cyprus Museum, Nicosia.*

and the manner of burial itself are evidence of this. The weapons, tools, ornaments, amulets and food that accompanied the body into the tomb also suggest the belief in an afterlife.

Death had to be approached with extreme caution, with a nice respect for its rites, in order to shield the living from its grim contagion and baleful influence.

At the very beginning of history, even in the Stone Age, one finds well-established rituals, handed down over the centuries from generation to generation. Thus, it has been suggested that the reason for burying the dead in a crouched, embryonic position was to prevent their shades from "walking" and returning to haunt the living. That is also why they were fittingly housed and bound or weighted down with stones.

But the precaution most likely to ensure peace for the living and the dead alike was scrupulous respect for the prescribed ritual. The corpse was protected and decked with ornaments and life-giving amulets, skeletons were stained with red ocher, the color of blood, the supreme agent of life, and shells were arranged about the body in a predetermined order. In some cases it was customary to cut off the head, the seat of strength, and eat the brain, in order to assimilate its magico-religious qualities.

In the Near East, during the fifth millennium, at the time of the transition from a life of hunting and gathering to a society based on agriculture and stock-raising, men began to turn their attention to the phenomena inherent in natural change. The succession of the seasons, the death and rebirth of vegetation, and the fecundation of the earth, the principal source of life, became primary religious preoccupations.

The interpretation of these mysteries had inevitable repercussions on the ceremonial associated with the worship of the dead. Statuettes of Venus made their appearance and the cult of the Great Goddess, symbol of the regenerative forces in nature, prevailed not only in Mesopotamia and Iran but also among the Megalithic civilizations of the Mediterranean and Western Europe (1).

Behind all this it is easy to discern the first efforts of a humanity, living under adverse and precarious conditions, to express its hopes and fears, first by means of a ritual technique, later by creating a mythology capable of satisfying its aspirations, providing the means of existence, fostering fertility and birth, and ensuring the survival of the dead.

Thus, concept became embodied in symbol, and the ritual apparatus became the visual expression of man's vital needs and their relation to the natural cycle. That is why, in their earliest manifestations, ritual, art and drama are linked together and make a common contribution to the birth of myth.

The stresses generated by the transformation of the way of life taking place in the Neolithic agricultural communities found emotional release in the contemplation of the succession of the seasons. A mythological form of the annual cycle came into being and eventually gave rise to the recorded rites of the calendar.

It is hardly surprising, then, that the beliefs and practices of the Near East and the Aegean, from the Paleolithic to the Bronze Age, should share so much in common, since they expressed

12   *BOWL WITH SPOUT.*   *Stone (andesite). Height: 10 cm, width: 30.5 cm.*
Neolithic I A (5800–5250 B.C.).   *Khirokitia (Larnaca).*   *Cyprus Museum, Nicosia.*

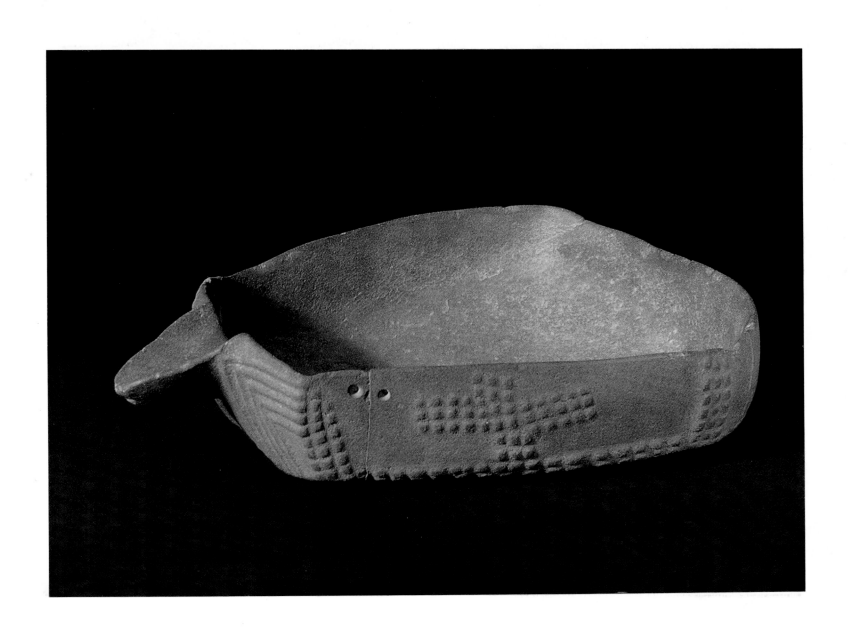

BOWL WITH SPOUT.   Stone (andesite). Height: 5 cm, length: 20.5 cm.
Neolithic I A (5800–5250 B.C.).   Khirokitia (Larnaca).   Cyprus Museum, Nicosia.

the fears and questionings of peoples living under similar conditions. Differences in myth and ritual between one region and another are due only to environmental differences that create distinctive needs and conditions of existence.

CYPRIOT RITUAL AND BELIEFS

During the Neolithic and the Bronze Age the Cypriot communities appear, in practice, to have shared the ritual and beliefs common to the general geographic area of which they formed part. In fact, excavations have revealed that their funeral customs were much the same as those that prevailed in other regions of the Neolithic world.

In Cyprus the worship of the dead is a cult of the greatest antiquity. At Khirokitia it was already in an advanced stage, which suggests preliminary phases of preparation and practices whose origin is to be sought beyond the limited horizons of the island itself.

The circular houses served as dwellings, but the dead were also buried beneath the floor, in a foetal position, with their knees drawn up to their chest. These tombs, though similar in type, are more recent than the ones found in Northern Mesopotamia and in Crete.

BOWL WITH SPOUT.   *Stone (andesite). Height: 17.8 cm.*
Neolithic I A (5800–5250 B.C.).   *Khirokitia (Larnaca).*   *Cyprus Museum, Nicosia.*

The need for veneration and the element of fear are also apparent. Thus, corpses have been discovered with stones laid on the chest or head. Primitive man was loath for the dead to return and haunt the living. For the same reason, stone vases and bowls were often deliberately broken before being disposed around the body. Animals and even children were sacrificed, in accordance with the customs of other Mediterranean societies, notably in Palestine.

The same ritual was still being followed at the end of the fourth millennium, as witnessed by various Chalcolithic tombs (Erimi, etc.).

The Bronze Age

In the Mediterranean the Bronze Age was an eventful period marked, in particular, by the mass migration of populations.

At a quite early date, there was a sudden change in burial practices. According to some theories, advanced by P. Dikaios and V. Karageorghis, the religious and funerary customs of the island were modified as a result of contact with Western Anatolia or the emigration of Anatolians seeking refuge in Cyprus after the catastrophe that had devastated their region.

This new civilization, quite distinct from the indigenous one, introduced its own rites and practices. The dead were buried not under the floor of the house, but in necropolises located away from the dwellings, usually on a hillside. The tombs were oval shafts dug out of the solid rock or formed in caves and were intended for entire families. This type of rock-cut tomb became general during the Bronze Age. As a rule, it consisted of a rectangular chamber approached by a passage (dromos) with or without steps. Another form of tomb (Early and Middle Bronze Age) had a dromos leading to a central chamber with lateral rooms in which offerings were placed.

The dead man, lying full length or crouched, was surrounded by many sumptuous presents to remind him of life. The archeologists have been singularly fortunate, particularly at Vounous, in unearthing exceptional finds so far unique in Cyprus. Apart from the usual vases and tools, they have found clay models representing the dead man's occupations – group scenes of dancing, sailing and tilling the land and, most important, an eloquent illustration of a religious ceremony (pages 30, 31). The grave goods often include richly ornamented bronze weapons (Vasilia), alabaster vases imported from Egypt, gold and silver jewelry, and pearl necklaces (Vounous), objects that bear witness to the affluence of a society in full economic and cultural bloom.

The sacrifice of domestic animals and human sacrifice continued to figure in the ceremonial ritual. In a warrior's tomb at Lapithos (tomb 5) the bodies lie face down, their hands tied behind their backs, firmly held by limestone slabs. The victims had been sacrificed during the funeral ceremony on a rectangular stone table pierced by a drainage channel for the blood which, seeping into the earth beneath, appeased the departed spirit.

Until Dikaios's discovery at Vounous (2) of the terra-cotta model of a temenos in which a ritual ceremony is being performed (pages 30, 31), our knowledge of the religious beliefs of the islanders was sketchy at best. In general, evidence dating mostly from the Late Bronze Age was relied upon to support theories relating to the practices of Cypriots of earlier periods.

Scenes represented on handsome sculptured vases provided occasional clues. Thus, it proved possible to guess the sacred nature of the bull and the existence of a chthonian cult devoted to the Serpent God, both of which are often represented in the incised decorative motifs and reliefs of the lustrous redware of the Early Bronze Age. The dual concept of the Mother-Goddess was found expressed in strange plaque idols in the form of a flat board with incised decoration.

These eminently agricultural societies based their beliefs on traditional ritual relating to the seasons and on vegetation myths. The divinities symbolizing fertility in animal form were primarily the bull and the serpent, everywhere present as powerful associates of the Mother-Goddess.

Other animals also occupied a distinctive place in the religious pantheon, as shown by the participation of individuals wearing bull's-head, stag's-head and sheep's-head masks in the sacred dances and religious ceremonies. By means of this disguise a sacramental relationship

BOWL WITH SPOUT.   *Terra-cotta. Combed ware. Height: 15 cm, width: 32.5 cm.*
Neolithic II A (3500–3200 B.C.).   *Khirokitia (Larnaca).*   *Cyprus Museum, Nicosia.*

HEAD OF IDOL.   *Stone. Height : 13.5 cm.*
Neolithic II A (3500–3200 B.C.).
Omodhos (Limassol).   *Cyprus Museum, Nicosia.*

was established between the man and the animal he represented – he identified with his adopted species in a spirit of communion.

The discoveries at the necropolis of Vounous confirmed these theories and illuminated many points that had previously been obscure. The ceremony illustrated by the model found by Dikaios takes place in a circular temenos, open to the sky, around three individuals standing close to the wall, facing the entrance. Serpents hang from their arms. Their backs are turned on a bas-relief depicting other bull's-headed personages, also holding serpents.

SEATED FIGURINE, WITH ARMS FORMING CROSS.   *Pale green steatite. Height : 15 cm.*
18   *Chalcolithic I (3000–2500 B.C.).*   *District of Paphos.*   *Cyprus Museum, Nicosia.*

It is known that the minotaurs belonged to the horde of demons in the service of the god, a persistent belief that reappears later in certain figurines of Ayia Irini. The bull's heads are attributes of the god of fertility, whereas the serpents, traditionally, are attributes of the hearth and of the god of fertility, but also represent a chthonian god.

According to Dikaios, who bases his conclusions on a study of this scene, the Earth-Mother had been worshipped since the Early Bronze Age in the form of the Goddess holding a child, as she is represented in the model. She was honored by associating her with the Serpent God and the Bull God. The latter was probably an agrarian deity, as indicated by another model showing a ploughing scene.

There is much additional evidence of the preeminent role played by these three divinities in the religious life of the island, for example, bowls decorated with "horns of consecration," of the sacred bull-serpent group, and horned figures holding serpents. One tomb, assumed to be that of a dancer priest, was even found to contain two terra-cotta horns, resembling those that he used in life.

Among the other figures in the temenos there are three more with their backs turned to the wall. To judge from the bull's-head masks worn by these three, the ceremony also included sacred dances, while another scene suggests that at some point live bulls were sacrificed.

Thus, there is every indication that this was a mystical ceremony restricted to initiates. The same conclusion may be drawn from the droll gesture of an individual who is trying to climb the walls to find out what is going on.

The ritual disclosed in this scene prompts one to reflect on the resemblances between the beliefs of the Cypriots and those of the Cretans and their probable common origin.

The Iron Age

During the Iron Age funerary architecture remained virtually the same, except for traces of Aegean influence, and indeed the form survived until the Roman period.

The arrival of the Mycenaeans on Cyprus in the course of the fourteenth century B.C., and particularly the Achaeans, who settled there one or two centuries later, led to important changes in beliefs, language and writing.

A new religion, involving different ceremonies and the worship of new gods, was probably founded.

The changes that took place on the island are well illustrated by a notable find at Enkomi (3), where two bronze statuettes, one of a young god wearing a conical horned cap (twelfth century B.C.) (page 77), the other, of later date, of a bearded god in a horned helmet, were unearthed, together with several two-headed centaurs in terra-cotta (eleventh century B.C.) and numerous bucrania.

The discovery of ox skulls and traces of libations in the central chamber of the temple where the young horned god was found and, not far away, of bull's horns and numerous ceremonial bowls proves that this statue was a cult object.

FIGURINE, WITH ARMS FORMING CROSS. Chalcolithic I (3000–2500 B.C.). *Pale green steatite. Height: 13 cm. Cyprus Museum, Nicosia.*

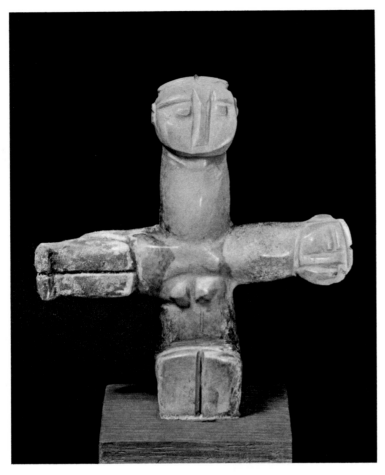

*SEATED FIGURINE, WITH ARMS FORMING
CROSS.*   *Steatite. Height: 9.3 cm.*
Chalcolithic I (3000–2500 B.C.).
Paphos.   *Cyprus Museum, Nicosia.*

It was, in all probability, the fertility god later called Apollo-Alasiotas or Keraetas (the horned one). According to a Greek inscription at Pyla (district of Larnaca) such a god was worshipped on Cyprus. Pausanias, who has left us such a valuable account of his wanderings in Greece, speaks of a temple in Arcadia dedicated to the "horned Apollo," the patron of cattle.

In view of the ties that existed between that region and Cyprus it is tempting to assume that the worship of this god was introduced by new colonists.

As for the second statuette, the "god of the ingot," recently found by Professor Cl.F.A. Schaeffer (4) in another sanctuary of the city, it appears to represent the divine patron of mines, a conclusion suggested by the fact that it stands on an ingot of copper.

The unfortunate gap in the archeological record between the eleventh and eighth centuries makes it impossible to trace the evolution of Cypriot beliefs during that obscure period. Presumably they gradually merged with those of the Greek peoples of the Aegean, while retaining traces of various oriental infiltrations, thus paralleling what is known to have happened in the domain of the arts.

Historically, Salamis came to the fore during the eleventh century B.C. Concerning the three centuries that followed, Cypriot archeology has almost nothing to report. No trace of

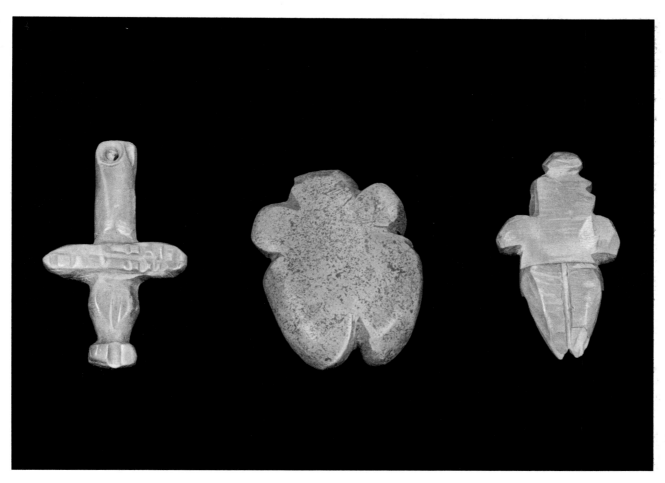

AMULETS.
Chalcolithic I (3000–2500 B.C.).

Steatite. From left to right. Height: 3.5 cm, 3.2 cm, 3.5 cm.
Cyprus Museum, Nicosia.

habitations, nothing but a few cemeteries. Hopefully, further excavations will provide the evidence required to close this serious gap. Those conducted so far (by P. Dikaios since 1957 and V. Karageorghis since 1962) on behalf of the D.A.C. (5) have been centered on a certain number of large tombs built during the eighth and seventh centuries.

The architecture is typical and speaks eloquently of the level of prosperity enjoyed by Cyprus at that time. A broad esplanade leads to a short stairway. Crossing a propylaeum, one enters the funerary chamber.

A simple effort of the imagination is enough to recreate the splendid funeral ceremony that was doubtless conducted in this imposing setting. The slow march of the escort, displaying for the last time the dead man's riches to the crowd, the procession of chariots followed by the distinguished pallbearers, musicians, and servants bearing offerings and personal belongings intended to make the afterlife more pleasant for their late master.

The ceremony unfolded in successive stages. First, the body, borne on a litter, adorned with precious jewels and richly appareled, was laid in its resting place; next, it was surrounded with the grave goods: vessels, eating and drinking utensils, weapons and toilet articles, lamps to light the long night. Then came ritual libations, banquets, and animal sacrifices. At Salamis skeletons of horses, their throats cut, have been found in situ, some still harnessed to their chariots. To cheer their long sojourn in the underworld, the dead needed company and servants. The Cypriots, like the Aegeans in general, were for the most part loath to practice human sacrifice. For living wives, servants, and musicians they substituted figurines and statuettes of washerwomen, flautists and cymbal players. To enable the dead to make their devotions, special attention was paid to statuettes of the Mother-Goddess whose power extended to the kingdom of the shades.

The human sacrifice detected in two tombs at Salamis, together with the sacrifice of horses, the burial of chariots, and the presence of large amphoras filled with oil and honey, suggests that funerary customs such as Homer describes in *The Iliad* were still being observed at that time (6).

The sanctuaries and temples of the Archaic period to be found on Cyprus are by no means as imposing as those of Greece and the Middle East. In general, they are small, modest structures characterized by a rustic simplicity.

A particularly important find (7) was the discovery of a twelfth-century sanctuary near the village of Ayia Irini. Originally open to the sky and surrounded by an enclosure, it underwent various transformations, reaching the peak of its importance between about 625 and 500, when it was destroyed in a flood and abandoned.

In its final form, consisting of an altar, a libation table, and two small chambers which, in all probability, were intended to shelter sacred trees, it may be compared with the small clay model of a temenos found at Vounous.

Spread around the altar were about 2,000 terra-cotta figures in a variety of styles. These have supplied valuable information on a number of obscure points. Other iron, bronze and ceramic objects, scarabs, etc., which help to flesh out the record, were also found.

The figurines, which vary in size from full-scale to miniatures, date from the final phase of the Cypriot Archaic period and tell a great deal about contemporary occupations, costume, and beliefs. They represent priests, worshippers, foot-soldiers, and charioteers armed with bows and shields and driving teams of centaurs and bulls. It is noteworthy that only two of the figures are female, which suggests that women were forbidden to enter the temple. A study of this material and the temple architecture reveals the persistence of certain religious ideas that had survived from the Bronze Age.

The sacrificial rites and dances, during which the officiating priests wore bull's-head masks, demonstrated the existence of a totemic bond between the man and the sacred animal.

The practice of zoolatry, very common throughout the Aegean, is also evidenced by the frequent presence in the tombs of doves and other animals, which were also reproduced on ceramics.

A seventh-century terra-cotta in the Louvre (donated by Declercq – H. de Boisgelin) representing a "Naiskos dedicated to Astarte" is most revealing in this respect. It depicts a religious ceremony in which three women perform a ritual dance to the sound of the lyre around a naiskos in the form of a dovecote. The Aegeans closely identified the dove with the

ASKOS, IN ANIMAL FORM. Black lustrous terra-cotta, incised decoration, incrusted with white slip.
Height: 15 cm, length: 20 cm.   Early Bronze I B (2200–2000 B.C.).   Cyprus Museum, Nicosia.

BOWL.   *Black lustrous terra-cotta, incised decoration, incrusted with white slip.*
Height : 6 cm, diam. : 12 cm.   *Early Bronze I B (2200–2000 B.C.).*   *Private collection.*

FLASK.   *Black-and-redware, incised decoration, incrusted with white slip. Height : 11.5 cm.*
Early Bronze I B (2200–2000 B.C.).   *Private collection.*

goddess of love and fertility, whose emanation it was. It was the spirit that sanctified everything it touched, animate or inanimate, and also the instrument of divine possession. It was adopted by Astarte at Hieropolis (8), and we know that the Minoans worshipped the Dove Goddess (9), as did the Pelasgians and the Chaldaeans.

It is possible to trace the communion between man and the animal divinity from Vounous, where it is manifested for the first time, through a second stage at Enkomi, where the horned-helmeted gods symbolize the idea of fertility associated with the attributes of the bull, a cult object of all primitive civilizations, representative of the male element responsible for the fertility of woman and the fruitfulness of the fields. The god takes the form of a bull the better to manifest his creative power and virility. In Crete, the man-animal was always a god, becoming the Minotaur, whose principal sanctuary was the palace of Minos itself. His is a very ancient cult, since he was already being symbolized by the "horns of consecration" during the Chalcolithic period (10).

GOURD-SHAPED VESSEL.   *Polished red-ware, incised decoration, incrusted with white slip.*
26 *Height : 34 cm.*   *Early Bronze I B (2200–2000 B.C.).*   *Cyprus Museum, Nicosia.*

Classical, Hellenistic, and Roman periods

During Classical, Hellenistic and Roman times contacts with Greece multiplied as a consequence of political adventures; religious beliefs were likewise affected and the Cypriots transferred their allegiance to the gods of the Hellenic pantheon, whose worship was common to the whole Greek world.

The ancient gods were henceforth identified with those of Olympus. All were worshipped with fervor, as witnessed by the monuments erected in their honor, the numerous epigraphic inscriptions in which they are invoked, and the statues that glorified their presence. None, whether god or demigod, was forgotten; all are there. But there were three, in particular, to whom the Cypriots were especially devoted.

The goddess of fertility was Hellenized and became Aphrodite. Born of the foam that gathered about the genitals of Uranus when Cronus threw them into the sea, her cult is mentioned by Homer (Odyssey VIII, 362). Source of inspiration to the first Cypriot poets, she remained the eternal symbol of beauty and love, Homer's Kypris, the uncontested queen of the island. Her temple near Paphos is considered one of the most famous temples of antiquity.

The worship of Apollo was also very popular; Kourion was the principal center, but his presence is keenly felt in other parts of the island, at Soloi where the epithets of "Kyptios" and "Lykios" were bestowed upon him, or at Kythrea where he was called "Hylates."

No less important was the Cypriot devotion to Zeus, "father of gods and men," who was worshipped in the great city of Salamis. Of his splendid temple there, built during Roman times, nothing but ruins now remains.

Various appellations that recur in the inscriptions ("Hypsistos," "Olympios," "Keraunios," etc.) tell of his power and the sentiments that his worship inspired.

Following the final annexation of Cyprus by Egypt (294 B.C.) under the Ptolemies, the dynastic cult was officially established. Starting from the reign of Ptolemy Epiphanes (203–181 B.C.) the sovereign took the title of High Priest and, following the deification of Arsinoe Philadelphis, often identified with Aphrodite, her worship spread throughout the island.

Even from this brief historical sketch of the customs and rites of the Cypriots it is clear that a close link existed between their beliefs and their art. To disregard this factor, magical or religious according to the epoch, the inspiration and source of many artistic manifestations, would be to renounce all hope of explaining or appreciating the spirit and the spirituality of Cypriot art. This character, originally dominant, is preserved even in its latest expressions, even after the penetration of new secularizing tendencies that might well have diverted the artist's attention.

The omnipresent religious influence stimulated and inspired sculpture, painting, and architecture. The sculptor modeled the body or the transposed image of the divinity. The painter

RITUAL VESSEL WITH LONG STEM.
Lustrous redware, incised decoration.
28 *Early Bronze I B (2200–2000 B.C.).*   *Vounous (Kyrenia).*
On the rim miniature animals and cups.
Height: 53 cm, diam.: 35 cm.
Cyprus Museum, Nicosia.

and the potter perpetuated the rites of the cult in their images and forms and depicted scenes from the divine mythology. Moreover, if we disregard the period when the Geometric style prevailed, from the moment that representational art reappeared it was again religious symbolism that predominated. The esthetic efforts of the builders were centered upon religious architecture. Artists were summoned to embellish the elegantly proportioned temples with mosaics and figures of the gods.

Art also derived inspiration from the rites and ceremonies performed in honor of the dead. The dead had to be given a fitting abode, assured of their existence in the beyond, and that dim existence had to be made more palatable by providing them with precious and useful objects that had given them pleasure in life; moreover, the presence of the gods was necessary to ward off evil spirits. At the same time, like the art of the Hellenes, Cypriot art, though suffused with religion, never accepted its constraints as submissively as the art of the Orient, where dogma imposed the motifs, directed the esthetic conception, and fixed or forbade forms and techniques. As W. Déonna has suggested in connection with Greek art (11), the explanation is to be sought in the fact that the island was never a theocracy. Moreover, the

MINIATURE MODEL OF A SACRED ENCLOSURE.   *Diam.: 37 cm.*
Early Bronze I B (2200–2000 B.C.).   *Vounous (Kyrenia).*   *Cyprus Museum, Nicosia.*

rationalism and the innate need for independence, so characteristic of the Cypriots, have always saved them from subservience to the dogmatists. However vital the influence of religion on art, the esthetic sense was always in control and prevailed over cult imperatives.

This conclusion can only be reinforced by a closer acquaintance with an art whose plastic beauty and originality can still be enjoyed and whose vicissitudes we are now about to trace through time.

THE ORIGINALITY OF CYPRIOT ART

A crossroads exposed to winds from every quarter, since the dawn of its history Cyprus has been a center of continuous activity where currents flowing from east and west have repeatedly crossed, mingled and merged.

Since the earliest antiquity the geographic position and natural resources of the island have caused it to be coveted and exploited by the great and powerful. Peoples and civilizations, converging upon it, now from the east, now from the west, encountered bitter local resistance. From these contending forces a new equilibrium was periodically established.

This, in brief, has been the history of the island called "macaria" (the happy), the "pleasant land," cradle of Aphrodite.

Cyprus, however, is not the simple symbol of the Anadyomene of Praxiteles; it is a living reality. Melting pot and catalyst of civilizations and cultures, during the centuries it has been able to sift out and assimilate the best of all these polymorphous contributions.

Hence that multivalent and contradictory art. Hence its essential originality. But the powers of discrimination displayed by the Cypriots necessarily imply an alert mind and a developed sensibility receptive to foreign influences.

The events that shook us out of our entrenched habits during the first decades of this century, by brushing aside the established principle of an intangible beauty, led us to revise our scale of values. Our esthetic conscience was prompted to seek satisfaction away from the beaten path of conformism, among primitive forms that disregard the so-called classical canons. Hence our taste for the art of Cyprus which, in certain phases, achieves the significance that we perceive in a genuine work of art.

There can be no doubt that we are by now well conditioned to grasp and appreciate the abundance of spirit displayed by the Cypriot artist, the richness of his invention, his lucidity and spontaneity of expression, the constants that at each instant recall his acceptance of constraints, but likewise his independence.

As soon as one begins to reflect upon the esthetic questions raised by the art of this island and tries to distinguish its special features, one is struck by the permanent elements that persist in spite of the changes dictated by evolution. Thus, the religious conscience, which

FEMALE PLAQUE IDOLS.   *Lustrous redware, incised decoration. From left to right.*
32   *Height: 23.8 cm and 22.7 cm.*   *Early Bronze I B (2200–2000 B.C.).*   *Cyprus Museum, Nicosia.*

FIGURINE OF A QUADRUPED.
Early Bronze I B (2200–2000 B.C.).

Lustrous redware, incised decoration. Length : 21 cm.
Cyprus Museum, Nicosia.

sustained and guided the spirit of the artists, at no time restricted their freedom to inquire into the mysteries and realities of life.

But Cypriot art could never have developed without the complicity of the natural surroundings which shaped the islanders' vision and influenced their behavior.

The gentleness of the temperate climate, without extremes of heat and cold, lightened the burden of finding food and shelter and dispelled the obsession with a latent menace, enabling men to seek pure enjoyment through the exaltation of their spirituality.

The bright sun and limpid light, by lending sharpness to the forms and throwing the masses into strong relief, invited the artist's hand to give his line a faultless clarity, to make the cleanly carved idols and the vigorous and austere contours of the statuary leap into space.

The open and accessible countryside and the call of the friendly sea fostered a spirit of discovery and tended to justify the acceptance of suggestions and the dissemination of ideas.

PITCHER. *Lustrous redware, incised decoration, incrusted with white slip. Height : 44 cm.*
34 *Early Bronze I B (2200–2000 B.C.).* *Episcopi (Limassol).* *Cyprus Museum, Nicosia.*

This combination of natural phenomena encouraged man to seize upon the essentials of whatever he observed. His appetite for life prompted him to view his surroundings with solicitude, led his imagination to invent new forms, and steered him away from the meticulous and servile reproduction of reality.

The evidence that has survived will enable us, in the course of this account, to verify these data which, together with the march of history, have dictated the laws of creation and the originality of expression of Cypriot art.

THE EARLY STAGES

THE DAWN OF A CIVILIZATION

When one finds oneself in the presence of a primitive civilization that has left only a fragmentary record behind, one's curiosity is all the keener because of the breadth of the unknown territory that the mind is left free to explore.

As one advances, the darkness recedes, hypothesis becomes supposition, supposition probability. The chain of deduction, with reality as its starting point, leads on to further speculation.

Thus, in the absence of written sources, the forms of the civil and religious architecture, objects, tools, and idols supply the initial data for reconstructing the thought, beliefs, philosophy, and mode of life of primitive societies.

The term "Neolithic" does not necessarily have any precise chronological connotation, but rather defines a cultural phase. Thus, the Early Neolithic of the Near East corresponds to the Middle Neolithic of Europe; the Late Neolithic of northwest Europe was coeval with the Bronze Age in the Near East.

The Neolithic was, above all, a time of transformation of the way of life, the age during which the farmer succeeded the hunter and the fisherman. An essential phase in the history of humanity, it brought fundamental changes in technology.

These changes were inspired by the demographic problem. In the course of millennia the population of the earth had multiplied, and men were now compelled to reverse their precious procedure. Up to then they had adapted themselves to the environment, practicing an "economy of depreciation," the destruction of resources. Henceforth they were to adapt the environment to their own needs, producing whatever was useful or necessary to their existence; hunting and gathering were supplemented by agriculture and stock-raising.

The beginnings of this crucial phase in human evolution, the diffusion of agriculture, have been traced to the Near East and to a time near the end of the Glacial Epoch when, as a result

MILK BOWL.   *Human and animal figures (cattle?) around the rim. Terra-cotta. Width: 48 cm.*
Early Bronze I B (2200–2000 B.C.).   *Margi (Nicosia).*   *Cyprus Museum, Nicosia.*

VESSEL WITH SPOUT. On the handle, a figure emptying a pot into a large vessel, probably a fermentation ceremony. Lustrous redware, incised decoration. Height: 32.8 cm. Early Bronze I B (2200–2000 B.C.). Cyprus Museum, Nicosia.

of drought, the forest lands and savannah grew dry and arid. These climatic changes drove men to seek out the valleys and mountain basins, areas with abundant game and vegetation, where water was still available.

The pursuit of agriculture, which necessitates a settled mode of life, gave new importance to the art of building, the use of polished flint tools, weaving, and pottery making. It prompted the growth of small permanent communities and the development of an elementary social structure. Existing beliefs were also transformed by the new imperatives. The worship of the dead

TERRA-COTTA PITCHER.   Modeled birds. Lustrous redware, incised decoration. Height: 26.5 cm.

Early Bronze I B (2200–2000 B.C.). Cyprus Museum, Nicosia.

39

became established in a cycle within which the idea of an afterlife persisted, but magic had yielded to myth. The peasant is governed by the natural phenomena of the succession of the seasons, which he tries to explain, appease and subdue. The stockbreeder is engrossed with the symbolism of strength and fecundity, with the virile male animal, the bull, the stallion, the he-goat.

The discovery of this new world led the artist to modify his vision. During the Paleolithic, the artist had tried to convey an almost expressionistic reality; during the Neolithic, his beliefs now being centered upon the spiritualization of natural forces, he tended to stylize his symbols.

Regardless of the reasons that induced him to apply such a technique, it is clear that he often tried to synthesize forms, to sublimate reality by shortcuts, simplifications, and bare outlines whose minimal features do no more than suggest the visible world.

THE NEOLITHIC PERIOD ON CYPRUS (5800–3000 B.C.)

In the Mediterranean basin Neolithic culture was sometimes spread by migration. This was probably the case with Cyprus where, so far at any rate, no evidence of an earlier local culture has been found. The funerary customs, the architecture of the dwellings, and the uniformity of the artefacts bear witness to a civilization already well advanced along the path of evolution. Although we can do little more than speculate about times so obscure, it seems probable that the first inhabitants of Cyprus were emigrants from Asia Minor who came to the island in search of better living conditions.

It was the Swedish Expedition of 1927–1931 that discovered a small number of sites belonging to a pre-Bronze Age civilization and thus established that the island had been inhabited in the very distant past.

Previously it had been thought that the first traces of a human presence dated back only to the third millennium, and the objects unearthed by the Swedes were initially assigned to the period from about 3700 to 3400 B.C. Further research between 1931 and 1935 (S.A.C.) brought the evolution of the Neolithic more fully to light. Carbon-14 tests pushed back the dates to the sixth millennium, when similar cultures existed in the Near East (Jericho, Jarmo, etc.) and in continental Greece.

Since then many sites have been discovered, so many, indeed, that there can be no doubt that even in those distant times the island supported a numerous population. Most of the dwellings have been found at the foot of hills near watercourses, where conditions were more favorable than on the wooded plains. A number of sites have been explored, but it is Khirokitia, Sotira, Kalavassos, and Erimi, in particular, that have been systematically excavated. This period was one of particular importance for the island. The archeological remains

PITCHER. *Decoration in relief. Lustrous redware. Height: 56 cm.*
40 *Early Bronze II (2000–1900 B.C.).* *Vounous (Kyrenia).* *Cyprus Museum, Nicosia.*

SMALL PITCHER, IN ANIMAL FORM.　　　*Pale orange-red terra-cotta, incised decoration. Height: 11.5 cm, width: 11.5 cm. Early Bronze II (2000–1900 B.C.). Priv. coll.*

attest the growth of a new civilization of Anatolian origin that must be regarded as one of the most ancient of the Mediterranean basin. Our knowledge of this civilization is derived mainly from the discoveries at Petra tou, Limniti, and Khirokitia.

Khirokitia

A recently nomadic people, some now herdsmen, others farmers, began to adapt themselves to village life. Like most Neolithic communities, this one consisted of a few dozen homes.

PITCHER WITH TRIPLE NECK.　　　*Lustrous redware, incised decoration. Height: 31 cm.*
Early Bronze II (2000–1900 B.C.).　　　*Cyprus Museum, Nicosia.*

The site, on high ground beside a stream not far from fields and woods, was chosen because it provided the necessary security and access to adequate sources of food.

So far, the excavations (12) have uncovered some fifty houses clustered on the side of a hill. But the little community must certainly have extended to several other knolls on the banks of the Maroniou river, which, though its own waters flow strongly only during the rainy season, is close to springs that never run dry.

The finds at Khirokitia have provided a basis for certain plausible conclusions and for a partial reconstruction of the social and religious customs and communal organization of its inhabitants.

It is well known that to each phase of civilization there corresponds a certain division of labor. To judge from more recent societies at the same technological level, it is probable that such activities as spinning and weaving, hoeing – the plow did not appear until the Bronze Age – pottery-making, and looking after the animals fell to the lot of the women. The men did the rougher jobs: they cleared the forest, hunted, cut stone and wood, and built homes.

Certainly, the Cypriot women must also have had such duties as grinding corn, preparing meals, and caring for the children (to judge from the twenty-five skeletons found within the walls of a single dwelling the mortality rate was very high).

Depending on the season, they had to lead the sheep to pasture or do the sowing and reaping. Wheat and barley, vegetables, flax and fruits were the usual crops in the Middle East and Europe at that time and some of them must also have been grown on Cyprus.

The elder women spun the flax and wove cloth. The men took their flint-headed weapons and roamed the woods and plains in search of game. The wild sheep and deer they stalked and killed supplied them with meat, warm skins, and horn for making tools and amulets.

Many objects have been found that bear witness to these occupations: grindstones, implements and vessels in obsidian, bone and stone, flint sickle blades and arrowheads, bone spindles and needles. The hours of leisure and relaxation were also used for carving bowls and idols in andesite, molding and decorating pottery, and making ornaments.

A civilization with artifacts as sophisticated as these could hardly have sprung into existence overnight. Thus it is by no means improbable that the future will reveal Mesolithic or Paleolithic sites linking this advanced culture with a more primitive past.

The finds

Those who examine the objects found in the tombs are often struck by their perfection of form, quality of workmanship, and functionalism. Carved in solid stone (andesite) with simple tools and limited means, they combine taste and utility with a rare discretion. The harmoniously curved shapes, pitted by the marks left by the pointed tool, have a rough surface that creates a lively play of light and shade. The well-proportioned spouts of the rectangular or round bowls and the ornamentation, incised or in stippled relief, of the smooth surfaces reveal the carver's love for his carving and an unmistakable esthetic intent (pages 9, 13, 14, 15).

LARGE MILK BOWL.   *Around the rim, four birds (doves?). Lustrous redware.*
44   *Total length: 65 cm.*   *Early Bronze I B (2100–2000 B.C.).*   *Cyprus Museum, Nicosia.*

BOAT-SHAPED PYXIS WITH RIDERS.   *White-painted terra-cotta. Height: 23.7 cm.*
Middle Bronze (1800–1600 B.C.).   *Vounous (Kyrenia).*   *Cyprus Museum, Nicosia.*

The same cannot be said for the ceramics. Toward the end of the Neolithic period technically advanced hand-shaped pottery appeared for the first time at Troulli on the north coast. The stratigraphic evidence shows that these were the first fruits of the period following the preceramic age. The rather crude decoration takes the form of red bands or diamond patterns on a uniform white field, a type that persisted into the Chalcolithic, when it became the dominant style.

Other objects, such as amber and dentalium necklaces, are evidence of the trading relations that must have existed between these first colonists and other communities able to supply them with the corresponding raw materials.

The idols

The artistic sense of the primitive craftsman is most evident in the modeling of his idols. Whereas his esthetic intentions are only casually reflected in the common utensils, by the addition of a decorative motif or the concern for a well-proportioned, slender or elegant form, these votive statuettes tell a different story.

PITCHER WITH DOUBLE SPOUT.   *White-painted terra-cotta. Height: 31.8 cm.*
Middle Bronze (1800–1600 B.C.).   *Lapithos (Kyrenia).*   *Cyprus Museum, Nicosia.*

Even in these early beginnings, when the carver struggled awkwardly to interpret his vision, one is struck by his innate sense of the balance of masses, the expressiveness of the hermetic features, and the imperious nudity of the figure (page 9). Other idols, representing animals treated with an astonishing boldness, confirm this indefinable but moving impression, not only by their air of modernity but also by all they convey of the accumulated questioning of the ages.

The terra-cotta heads of similar date (page 10), though cruder in treatment, breathe the same aura of mystery. The appeal to our sensibilities is the same. The round flattened head with features in low relief and the enigmatic face with hollow eyes fixed on infinity are just as curiously provocative, though less peremptory and more clandestine in their manner of achieving this effect.

Fifteen centuries separate the first Neolithic age from the second, fifteen centuries of total obscurity, since no sites have been found that might help to bridge the gap. Exactly what happened during those missing years there is no means of telling. H.W. Catling has suggested that the island may have been abandoned in the wake of some catastrophe (13), but this is no more than a risky and totally unsupported hypothesis.

Excavations made in 1947 and 1950 (P. Dikaios at Kalavassos and Sotira (14), for the D.A.C. and the Museum of Pennsylvania) revealed the presence of new dwellings. The architecture and funerary customs were different from those of the preceding civilization. But the principal innovation was a type of pottery known as combed ware, probably of Palestinian origin and remarkable not only for the maturity of the treatment but also for its specific character (page 17).

The prehistoric site of Sotira, most of which has been excavated, is perched on a steep hill. Some of the houses are circular, in the same style as those at Khirokitia, but others, rectangular in plan with rounded corners, are of a type previously unknown. At Kalavassos the shaft dwellings are partly dug out of the rock. They were originally topped by a light roof of plastered canes supported in the middle by a post.

The dead were no longer buried beneath the floor of the house but in the open, close by the village, which implies a more advanced stage in the evolution of religious beliefs.

Apart from stone objects and flint and bone implements, which continued in use, combed pottery appeared, especially at Kalavassos. The jars, which are sometimes quite large, and the round or spouted bowls in the Anatolian tradition are covered with a dark-brown semi-lustrous clay slip to reduce the porosity. The decoration, applied with a comb before firing while the slip was still fresh, consists of bands of straight or undulating lines (perhaps in imitation of the motion of the waves) (page 17).

Despite its crudeness and a certain clumsiness of treatment, this early local pottery already displays a quite developed sense of artistry. The interpretation of forms and decoration is undoubtedly foreign in origin, but has been enriched by the Cypriot sense of order and balance and feeling for ornamental motifs. The geometric decoration of the handsome

VESSEL IN THE FORM OF A BULL. Lustrous redware, incised decoration. Height: 13 cm, length: 16.3 cm. Early Bronze III (1900-1800 B.C.). Soloi (Nicosia). Cyprus Museum, Nicosia.

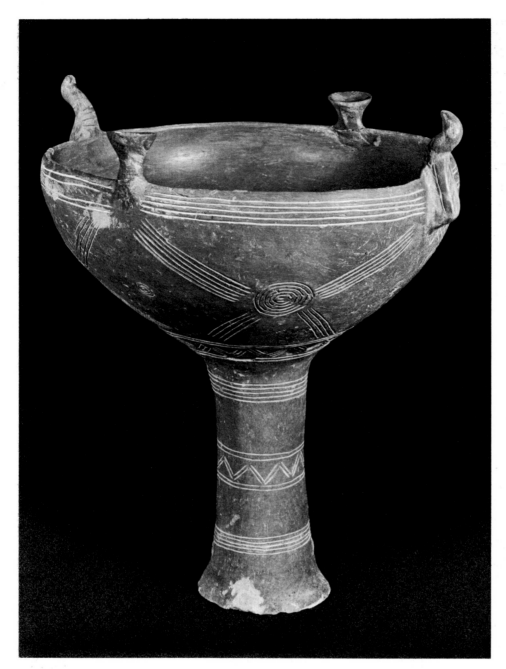

VESSEL WITH STEM. Around the rim, animals and cups. Lustrous red-
ware, incised decoration.   *Height: 28.5 cm, diam.: 22.5 cm.*
Early Bronze III (1900–1800 B.C.).   *Cyprus Museum, Nicosia.*

surfaces was to be more methodically and systematically applied during the Chalcolithic. The void that separates the two documented periods of the Neolithic poses insoluble problems with regard to the evolution of the arts. In the absence of a complete chain of evidence, one would be rash indeed to advance hypotheses that might be contradicted by subsequent discoveries. It is true, however, that the tradition of stone sculpture and the craft of modeling in clay were by now well established.

COMPOSITE PITCHER.   *Lustrous redware, incised decoration. Height: 42.5 cm.*
Early Bronze III (1900–1800 B.C.).   *Hubbard Collection, Kyrenia.*   *Cyprus Museum, Nicosia.*

The stone idol's head reproduced on page 18 has been worked in the same way as before, but the style has evolved in the direction of a deliberate simplification in which all traces of realism are effaced. The eyes and the nose are barely indicated, in the lightest of relief. But what is even more remarkable is the extreme elongation of the neck, a form that persisted into the Chalcolithic.

This piece with its closed, inscrutable beauty, the expression of a human adventure that hurls defiance at time, captures among the immense range of invented forms that particular style that gives pleasure while subtly involving us in its own strange world.

Certain very realistic terra-cotta heads and others that seem to have been made to be impaled on banners or poles have a workmanlike bluntness that contrasts strangely with the refined products of the stone-carvers.

THE CHALCOLITHIC PERIOD (3000–2300 B.C.)

The Chalcolithic period, which spanned seven centuries, marked the transition from stone to metal and is characterized by the simultaneous production of objects made of copper (chalcos) and ceramics.

The excavations conducted by P. Dikaios for the Department of Antiquities of Cyprus (henceforth D.A.C.) at various sites (Kalavassos B, Ambelikou, Erimi) between 1933 and 1953 and by T. Hatkins at Philia-Drakos in 1965 throw a certain amount of light on this otherwise obscure epoch.

Local migrations
At the beginning of the third millennium the Neolithic populations were somehow displaced and abandoned their original settlements in favor of other parts of the island. Our knowledge of these events is still too incomplete for us to piece together exactly what happened, but, whatever the reason for these local migrations, they must have upset established customs and created new living conditions appropriate to the new environment. One possible explanation is a natural catastrophe that affected only part of the island. But this is no more than a supposition.

Living conditions
To judge from the numerous sites discovered, the island appears to have been well populated in those times. The growth of the population presupposes an increase in agricultural production, which must certainly have given rise to some form of social reorganization. Thus the progressive differentiation of skills must have led some people to give up agriculture for commerce and the various crafts. The discovery of copper deposits can only have brought an

PLAQUE IDOL, nose in relief. Lustrous redware, linear decoration incised on both faces. Height: 26 cm. Early Bronze III (1900–1800 B.C.).   Hubbard Collection, Kyrenia.   Cyprus Museum, Nicosia.

53

AMPHORA.   *Terra-cotta. Height : 21.2 cm.*
Middle Bronze II–III (1750–1600 B.C.).
Amathus (Limassol).   *Musée d'Art et d'Histoire, Geneva.*

intensification of the exchanges with neighboring peoples inaugurated during the previous period.

Both at Erimi and at Karavas, on the north coast, the funerary customs continue the tradition of Khirokitia, although in a more relaxed vein.

It is impossible, from these faint clues, to establish the successive stages which, with the slow passage of time, marked the gradual advance of these burgeoning societies. What we

PITCHER.   *White-painted terra-cotta. Height : 34 cm.*
54   *Middle Bronze II (1750–1700 B.C.).*   *Lapithos (Kyrenia).*   *Cyprus Museum, Nicosia.*

have are only occasional milestones scattered somewhat at random along the road, at best enough to define the material level, but inadequate to reveal the exact significance of the sequence of cultures.

The replacement of stone by pottery

A distinct improvement in the way of life is apparent from the evidence of the excavations. The use of stone for domestic articles was almost completely abandoned in favor of pottery. The ceramics, found in abundance more or less everywhere, are remarkable for their variety and the inventiveness of the decoration. Stone and flint implements continued in use, but they were more numerous and more diversified in function. Moreover, copper utensils made their first appearance.

Erimi

It is Erimi that best illustrates this intermediate phase leading to the Bronze Age, where the record is much fuller and more conclusive.

The site is close to Limassol, in the south of the island, with a certain number of dwellings built in a hollow in the stony terrain. The houses are of the "tholos" type, similar to those at Khirokitia, but with a different superstructure, like that of Sotira.

Red-on-white ware

A distinguishing feature of the Erimi civilization is its "red-on-white" pottery with the motifs painted in orange or red over a pale slip background. Both the technique and the style show evidence of knowledge acquired by a long experience or passed on by tradition. Otherwise it would be difficult to account for such an abrupt change. Only the discovery of a site inhabited continuously from the Neolithic to the Bronze Age would make it possible to trace the various phases of development leading to this already highly advanced style.

It is the creative process, the conception that is new, the problems involved that are differently formulated. Certainly, the potter commanded a more impressive array of technical skills, but it is, above all, his manner of thinking and seeing that has evolved. The primitive Neolithic man, ruled by instinct and feeling, has given way to the logician. Having abandoned the still rudimentary methods of combed decoration, he has frequently moved on to a studied composition.

This abstract geometrism with its strictly disciplined lines, the surfaces punctuated with repetitive fish or leaf shapes between intercrossing bands, even the less common stylized floral motifs, so flexible and so exuberant, bear witness to a surprising level of skill and freedom of spirit. So accomplished a style does not appear again until a much later date.

This decoration ("red-on-white"), although the most prevalent, was not the only kind to be employed. Both at Erimi and elsewhere (notably Ambelikou) pottery of the variety known as "lustrous red or black ware" has been found in lesser quantities, together with other types.

FLAGON WITH DOUBLE NECK AND SPOUT. White-painted terra-cotta. Height: 34 cm.
Middle Bronze II (1750-1700 B.C.). Lapithos (Kyrenia). Cyprus Museum, Nicosia.

FIGURINES OF NUDE WOMEN.   *Terra-cotta. From left to right. Height: 17.9 cm and 17 cm.*
Middle Bronze (1800–1600 B.C.).   *Cyprus Museum, Nicosia.*

As for the forms, their evolution is, admittedly, closely linked with parallel advances in cultural development, but they no longer remain restricted to the traditional examples of Khirokitia. Though the latter continued in use, new forms were invented: for example, pitchers derived from models suggested by gourds and other household articles formerly made of skin. Though he still lacked the wheel, the potter's remarkable skill is apparent in the thinness of the walls and in the dimensions of the vessels he produced: milk bowls, jars and pitchers, whose forms, sometimes of an inspired elegance, were to reach their fullness of perfection during the Bronze Age.

First occurrence of copper

Though the ceramics of Erimi are highly characteristic of this phase of Cypriot civilization, there are other indications of the progress that had been made. In fact, the first use of metal

must date from around the third millennium. This is attested by the discovery, in a village near Ambelikou, of a crucible bearing traces of molten copper, together with molds probably intended for making adze heads for chipping wood. A chisel, found at Erimi and now on display in the Nicosia Museum, provides the first evidence of the use of pure wrought copper, justifying the name "Chalcolithic" for this period.

This new activity was certainly not unconnected with the development of trading relations with Anatolia, which had expanded remarkably during the preceding centuries. The technique of working in metal must have been borrowed from the Asians, if one recalls that the craftsmen of Byblos, Egypt and Mesopotamia were already highly skilled in the art. Other sources also throw light on the increasing contacts with the outside world. Thus there are certain resemblances between Cypriot pottery and that of Syria, Palestine, or even Thessaly. The flint objects and ornaments likewise suggest comparisons with the similar work of neighbors to the east and west.

Statuettes

The modeling and artistic conception of the statuettes is another source of surprise, to which our modern eyes are particularly sensitive. Certainly, the material employed, steatite, imposed its own laws on the craftsman, while offering him possibilities that he had previously been denied. Easily worked, it lends itself more readily than stone to the modeling of plastic forms.

Magic, whose dominion must certainly have extended to this primitive art, subjected it to the rules of an abstract symbolism. Naturalism was discarded, the statue became simplified, stylized and almost two-dimensional, in some ways anticipatory of the flat idols of the Bronze Age. The neck is elongated, cylindrical; the outflung arms balance the symmetry of the whole. The face is flattened and the simple outlines of the features are lightly raised or hollowed out. The wide eyes are focused on infinity in a time-defying gaze (pages 19, 21, 22).

These pale-green or deep-black figurines with their mat surfaces are the product of an ideographic vision of the body. The stark delineation of the features and the simplified transition from the plane to the curve, achieved not by antitheses but by a refinement of the modeling consisting in an elongation of the neck and arms, are the work of an artist who has withdrawn into a world of speculation far removed from all reality. It is clear that a new world has come into being, a search for a rationality whose guiding principles elude its means of action. We are ignorant of the function of these statuettes. Were they idols, votive offerings, or talismans (page 23)? Did they accompany the dead on their journey into the beyond or did they symbolize a god?

Although there are examples of indeterminate sex (page 21), most of the figures are female. Moreover, the typology is related to that of the Mother-Goddess common to the entire Mediterranean basin.

PYXIS, IN ANIMAL FORM.
Middle Bronze III (1700–1600 B.C.). *White-painted terra-cotta. Height: 14 cm, length: 22 cm.* *Hubbard Collection, Kyrenia.* *Cyprus Museum, Nicosia.*

SCULPTED VESSELS (RHYTONS), IN ANIMAL FORM.   *Terra-cotta. Base ring ware.*
From right to left. Length: 15.3 cm, height: 11.5 cm.
Late Bronze II (1400–1230 B.C.).   *Cyprus Museum, Nicosia.*

BRONZE-AGE CIVILIZATION

General remarks

During the Bronze Age, one of the most important stages in the evolution of mankind, living conditions were radically transformed by the acquisition of the ability to work in metal. The transition from a stone to a bronze technology took time, and the nature of the change was not everywhere the same. But there can be no doubt that the experience acquired by Neolithic man in the cutting and working of stone stood him in good stead when his attention was drawn to the similar possibilities of metal.

It is assumed that he first observed, more or less by chance, that native copper could be hammered into various useful shapes. The next step was to roast and smelt copper and tin in stone-walled furnaces and cast ingots that could be stored and later exported or turned into weapons and tools. Many long years must have intervened, however, between the initial discovery and the organization of the first efficient foundries. It may be that on Cyprus the process was accelerated, since contacts with eastern communities, skilled in the metal-working arts, had continued uninterrupted since the earliest antiquity.

BOWL WITH SPOUT.
Late Bronze I A–I B (1600–1400 B.C.).

White-painted terra-cotta. Width: 37.5 cm.
Cyprus Museum, Nicosia.

Besides introducing lustrous red ware, the colonists arriving from Anatolia in the third millennium also brought with them the metal-working techniques which, it seems, the Mesopotamians were the first to master.

Such were the profits that flowed into the Cypriot mining areas that their inhabitants were prompted to imitate the opulent mode of life enjoyed abroad, although conditions in general were still relatively backward.

It is known that once the mines of Sinai were exhausted, Cyprus gained the reputation of the greatest exporter of copper to the eastern Mediterranean. Suddenly, the islanders were rich. In exchange for their minerals, timber and ceramics, they demanded Egyptian horses and chariots and from the Aegeans, and especially the Cretans, manufactured goods. A magnificent bronze vase found at Episcopi could only have been engraved by a skilful Cretan artist of the late Mycenaean age.

The few copper objects produced during the preceding phase were harbingers of the important evolution and metamorphosis that the civilization of the island was to experience during the next thirteen centuries. This long period witnessed a succession of crucial events with direct or indirect repercussions on Cypriot social structures, beliefs, cultural development and art.

Populous and endowed with important natural resources, Cyprus attained a high level of prosperity by pursuing trade. A bridge linking the Aegean with Egypt and Asia, a strategic center and source of raw materials, Cyprus was envied and exploited by the great and powerful. Its destiny was shadowed by the confrontation of two worlds, East and West. Three events dominate its early history: the peaceful penetration of the Anatolian tribes; the Pharaonic conquest; and the Mycenaean colonization followed by the Achaean invasion, which ended in the total Hellenization of the island.

EARLY BRONZE AGE OR EARLY CYPRIOT (2300–1800 B.C.)

Our knowledge of the Early Bronze Age is far from complete. Of those long centuries, which include the last phase of the Chalcolithic, only a fragmentary record survives, though so far, it is true, none of the numerous scattered sites has been systematically excavated and most of the information we do possess has been extracted from the tombs. The few remains at Ambelikou and a dwelling at Alambra give only a faint idea of the contemporary architecture.

Under the pressure of population growth new areas were colonized. Unlike the early Neolithic settlers who had clung to the coast, the Bronze-Age Cypriots, probably impelled by new needs, began to penetrate the interior.

The pastoral life continued, side by side with agriculture and forestry. But these occupations were now joined by a fourth – copper mining. Unfortunately, we know scarcely anything of the successive stages in the exploitation of the natural resources of the island. Was it the ready availability of metal that attracted the newcomers who arrived about 2300 B.C.? They would have come from the west coast of Anatolia, having been forced to flee their native country as a consequence of the catastrophe that engulfed it at about that time. This migration of tribes from the shores of Asia, though peaceful, caused Cyprus to shed some of its insularity and won it a new place in the international quorum. A special Anatolian accent was preserved throughout the Bronze Age, being gradually assimilated by the native Cypriot elements.

The new colonists brought with them all the skills that they had acquired from other more advanced peoples and a process of cultural osmosis developed between the natives and the immigrants. The changes in burial customs, religious rites – as exemplified by the famous discovery (at Vounous, see page 10) of a clay model of a temenos (pages 30, 31) – domestic and religious architecture, and, above all, artistic expression, are convincing proof of this.

The encroaching allogeneous civilization, herald of an era of progress, has been fully documented by the exploration of the region of Philia (D.A.C., 1943). On the fringes of the bay of Morphou, facing Asia, it was a convenient point of disembarkation for the new arrivals.

PITCHER (copy of metal jug).
Late Bronze I A–I B (1600–1400 B.C.).

Terra-cotta. Base ring ware. Height: 46.5 cm.
Cyprus Museum, Nicosia.

JUG, AMPHORA, PITCHER *(copies of metal vessels).*
From right to left. Height: 15.5 cm, 11.6 cm, and 17.5 cm.
Late Bronze I A–I B (1600–1400 B.C.).

Terra-cotta. Base ring ware.

Cyprus Museum, Nicosia.

The Anatolians did not stop at the coast, however, but gradually pushed into the interior (Ayia Paraskevi near Nicosia and Vasilia in the district of Kyrenia), even reaching Anoyira and Sotira on the south coast and Vasilia in the north.

Pending the discovery of inhabited sites, our only data are the grave goods found in tombs. These include the products of a civilization different from the native one. Thus, side by side with ceramics in the local style, new forms appeared, such as the flat-bottomed, slender-necked, lipped vase and black-slip combed ware of distinctly Anatolian origin (page 26).

Ceramics

At first (civilization of Philia) the potter resisted the innovations introduced by the new arrivals. He clung to his rather unpolished style of simplified geometric decoration painted in red on a white ground, continuing the tradition of Chalcolithic art.

It took a century for the change to become apparent, the initial reticence gradually yielding to the later fashion. Increasing contacts with the mainland certainly did much

PITCHER.
Late Bronze II (1400–1230 B.C.).

Terra-cotta, white slip I. Height: 22 cm, width: 7.5 cm.
Cyprus Museum, Nicosia.

to tip the scales by legitimizing the acceptance of new suggestions. These contacts are attested by the presence in the tombs (necropolis of Vounous) of Syrian vessels, copper necklaces and knives, previously unknown on Cyprus, and other objects of oriental inspiration.

Sculptured vases

This stylistic modification or modernization was achieved, in particular, by adapting the prototypes to local requirements. Thus, the shapes of the lustrous vases of Anatolian origin were progressively refined. The necks grew longer, the silhouette acquired a certain elegance, imagination contributed to the enrichment of the incised ornament (page 25), and the newly introduced plastic decoration or relief prompted an unexpected display of motifs caught, as it were, on the wing. The ceremonial vases have been modeled with particular care and reflect the religious fervor that must have animated these primitive craftsmen. The earliest known example of this treatment, so characteristic of the epoch, is a wide-mouthed ritual vessel supported on a tall pedestal. A zigzag pattern is symmetrically incised in the red slip, while three small cups and three animal figures are distributed in a rhythmic sequence around the rim (page 29).

The latter part of this phase (2100–2000 B.C.), chiefly documented by the excavations at the necropolis of Vounous (Cyprus Museum and the Louvre, 1931–1933), is certainly the richest in imaginative force and most informative with regard to the process of assimilation of the advances made in earlier periods.

No resource was neglected. Everything became enriched: the play of forms, the exuberance of the decoration, the inventiveness of the plastic motifs. The borrowings were absorbed and transmuted into a purely Cypriot style of striking originality. The artist broke free of the former logic, designed exclusively to serve the needs of an elementary functionalism. His esthetic intentions are obvious. The simple stage of everyday connivances and religious preoccupations has been left far behind. The need for independence from Oriental prototypes and the urge to affirm a sound original conception are suggested by the very image of the objects. Thus, the flat base of the bowls and pitchers tends to disappear, replaced by the sensual sweep of the curve. At other times, the craftsman is impelled to make his work soar, pruning away the form until it tapers to a conical point. He retains the lustrous red patina for the sake of its surface effects, though a little later he was not to disdain the white background, a resurgence of the Chalcolithic style, against which the design can be more emphatically displayed.

The forms are highly varied, no longer subject to a fixed rule or canon. Without losing the general characteristics appropriate to each type of object (milk bowls, pitchers, goblets, pyxes, etc.), they developed into a multitude of variants, with a tendency to increasing complexity. Thus, the imitation of a gourd, a new device, might be repeated three or four times on the same vase (page 51).

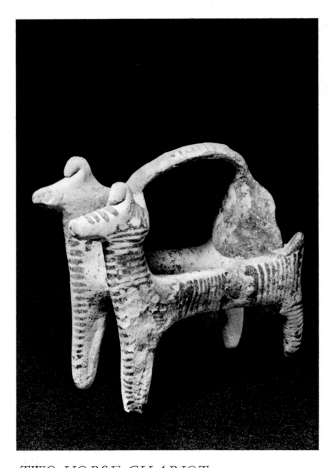 

TWO-HORSE CHARIOT.
Terra-cotta.   *Height : 9.6 cm., length : 11 cm.*
Mycenaean period (1400–1200 B.C.).
Cyprus Museum, Nicosia.

BOWL WITH SPOUT AND BULL.
Terra-cotta.   *Height : 9.5 cm.*
Minoan period (eighteenth century B.C.).
Karmi.   *Cyprus Museum, Nicosia.*

But it is the ornament, incised, in low relief or in the round, that reveals the full measure of the artist's talent. It abounds in individual figures, symbolic animals, birds, and more elaborate vignettes, in which the taste for narrative is apparent. These scenes are even repeated in clay as independent compositions (tilling the fields, religious ceremonies, etc., see pages 30, 31).

The plaque idols

The demands of magic and religion, though they could not be satisfied by mere functionalism, did not exclude esthetic pleasure. The unusual flat idols with decoration incised on a lustrous red ground, which in some respects recall the stone idols of the Neolithic (page 9), are evidence enough of this.

These figurines deserve more than a cursory glance. Their function is not in doubt. They accompanied the dead on their long journey into the other world, as substitute images to function in the dead man's place.

As far as I know, they are a phenomenon unique in art, with no parallels except in our century, and even there the parallelism is simply in the artist's vision, with no question of a formal analogy.

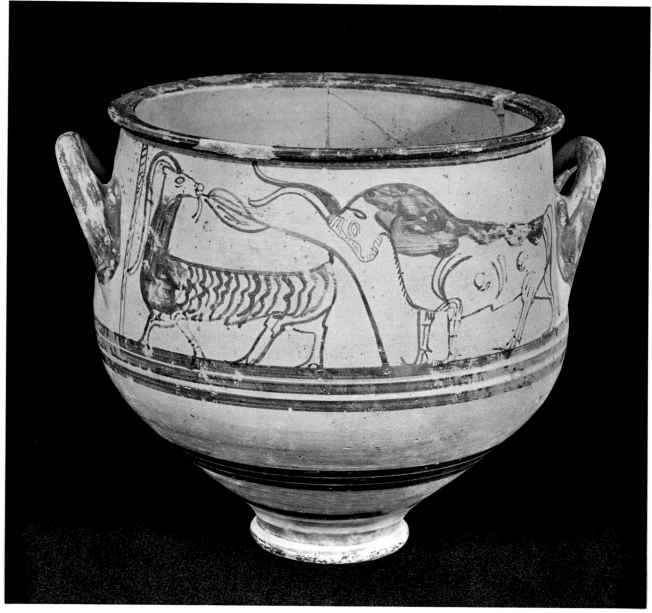

KRATER.
Mycenaean III B (1300–1230 B.C.).　　　Enkomi (Famagusta).　　　Terra-cotta. Height: 28.7 cm.
Cyprus Museum, Nicosia.

In any case, they confront the esthetician with multiple and contradictory problems that defy satisfactory elucidation. Indeed, how can one explain this radical swing from the modeled to the flat form, from the plastic to the two-dimensional? Were there intermediate steps that the excavations have not yet revealed?

The flatness of the idols is an innovation. It expresses an extraordinary boldness on the part of the artist. The form was never to appear elsewhere, nor did it reappear on Cyprus once the Late Bronze-Age artist had gone back to modeling in the round, drawing inspiration from the Mother-Goddess dear to the Orientals (Babylon, Syria, Western Asia).

Esthetically, these strange idols have two distinguishing characteristics. On the one hand, there is the highly schematized representation of reality, the unconditional adherence of the artist to a formal purism, the return to "primary forms," to use the current jargon. Thus, the

71

body is only sketchily delineated, being framed by a large rectangle that supports a second narrower rectangle representing the neck and face. There is no trace of feet. As for the other features, the existence of arms, breasts and rudiments of the face (ears, eyes, nose, mouth) is cursorily acknowledged, merely suggested in low relief or by shallow incisions.

At the same time, it is clear that the artist was also motivated by a concern for realism in his rendering of such details as ornaments, necklaces, and the decoration of the clothing.

In general, the first impression is one of a "primitive" conception. The vision of the artist has the same naïveté as that of a child who expresses himself by eliminating the superfluous to get at the essentials. The presumption is that the artist lacked technical skill, but, in my opinion, this is a facile conclusion that is, in any case, invalidated by the parallel existence of plastic and three-dimensional animal figures that already demonstrate a mastery of advanced techniques (pages 25–29). Now, the deliberate limitation to only two dimensions, the stylization, and the elaborate engraved decoration can only be explained in terms of the function that the idols were intended to perform. This self-imposed restraint, probably inspired by religious or at least magical considerations and embodying some idea or myth of Neolithic society, appears to have been maintained for a certain period, but was then relaxed for reasons that remain obscure. This, however, is no more than a guarded hypothesis, since supporting evidence that might throw further light on the problem is totally lacking.

At the same time, such speculation has nothing to do with the artistic value of the idols which remains intangible and unique. Whatever the explanation may be, the creative mystery that surrounds these modest products of simple craftsmanship will not easily be penetrated.

Other objects

There is other evidence of the degree of evolution and prosperity of Cypriot civilization at this time, in addition to the abundant pottery and anthropomorphic terra-cottas.

The transformation of industry was not the simple result of an internal evolutionary cycle, but a consequence of the rising tide of cultural exchanges and movements of peoples that was stirring the contemporary world. This is attested by the variety of grave goods found in the tombs.

Copper and bronze tools and weapons became more plentiful and more diversified, which suggests advanced technical knowledge and the existence of metal-working shops. The famous Cypriot dagger with the long willow-leaf blade was the principal product of the copper industry. It was widely exported and highly prized by the neighboring Anatolians.

Moreover, female love of finery was no longer to be satisfied with crude ornaments. Foreign contacts brought changes in taste and fashion. The Phoenician sailors, shrewd traders, certainly engaged in barter and offered jewelry in exchange for metal. It is enough to mention the rich array of gold and silver jewelry found at Lapithos, including ornaments and spirals for wearing in the hair and white and green faience-pearl necklaces, doubtless of Egyptian origin.

KRATER.
Mycenaean III·A (1400–1300 B.C.).

Terra-cotta. Height: 37.5 cm.
Cyprus Museum, Nicosia.

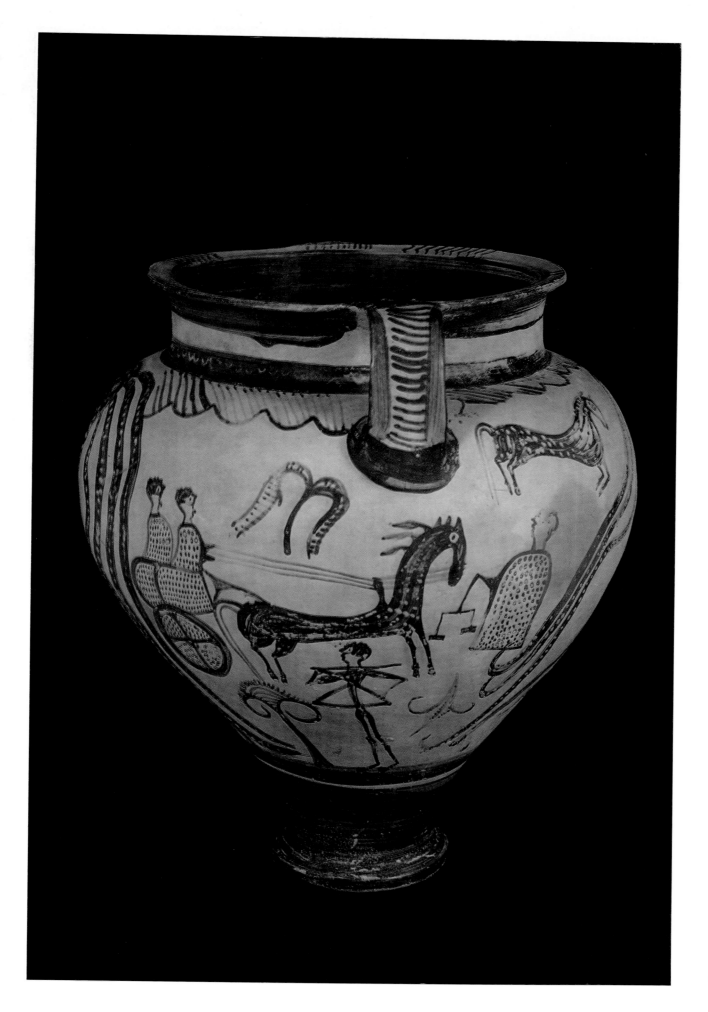

MIDDLE BRONZE AGE OR MIDDLE CYPRIOT (1800–1600 B.C.)

In the East, this phase of the Bronze Age, though it lasted only a relatively short time, was marked by events of the first importance.

Whereas in Europe populations were becoming stabilized, the countries of the Aegean, like Anatolia, Egypt, Mesopotamia, and Iran, were experiencing an era of internal disorder and incursions.

This was the period during which the Hittites founded their kingdom in Cappadocia (about 1775) and Hammurabi, king of Babylon, unified Mesopotamia, giving it an elaborate administrative and political structure, as well as a highly developed system of laws (the famous code of Hammurabi). The decadence of royal power in Egypt led to a weakening of the frontier defenses and the fall of the country to the Hyksos, a warrior clan from Syria whose victories depended on their effective exploitation of two recent military innovations: the deployment of squadrons of horse-drawn chariots, a tactic first evolved in Mesopotamia, and the use of the lance and javelin.

It was also the period during which Cretan civilization reached its apogee. The products of its workshops, notable for their technical perfection and refined taste, soon won the favor of the Syrians and Phoenicians, and Ras Shamra-Ugarit became one of the principal ports of call for the Cretan traders. Relations with Cyprus, which straddled this route, were also developed, as evidenced by the Minoan vases and metal tools found on the north coast of the island. However, in about 1700 Crete suffered a great catastrophe that destroyed its finest palaces. At about the same date the Achaeans descended on Greece.

This continuous mingling of tribes and civilizations, with its sad corollary of wars, invasions and civil conflict, created an atmosphere of instability that was not without its effect on Cyprus.

International relations

At that time Phoenicia was a natural center for the distribution of raw materials, in exchange for which it could offer both manufactured goods and agricultural products. To Byblos its ships brought not only Bactrian lapis lazuli and Sudanese ebony but copper from the Caucasus and Cyprus, not to mention Lebanese resin and cedarwood for which the principal market lay in Egypt. In return, the Phoenicians supplied their neighbors with cloth, weapons, jewelry, and foodstuffs. Syrian and Palestinian traders began to appear in ever-increasing numbers on the Cypriot shores and the regions in the south and southwest, more conveniently located for the purposes of international trade, began to flourish at the expense of the areas where the northern clans had recently known such splendor.

Historical events

Our knowledge of this period is still uncertain, being mostly based on tomb finds and the remains of early military architecture. The single house, part of an urban complex, excavated

RHYTON.
Mycenaean III B (thirteenth century B.C.).   *Kition.*

Faience. Height: 26 cm.
Cyprus Museum, Nicosia.

at Kalopsidha can give no more than a fragmentary idea of the domestic architecture. A large structure, it comprised eleven rooms built around a rectangular court.

On the other hand, the numerous fortified sites dating from the seventeenth and sixteenth centuries (at Ayios Sozomenos, Nicolidhes, in the center of the island, Nitovikla, on the slopes of the Kyrenia mountain range, and particularly Krini) and their destruction, like that of Enkomi toward the middle of the sixteenth century, speak of the troubled times through which the native populations must have passed.

The causes of these events escape us. Were they directly or indirectly connected with the conquest of Egypt by the Hyksos, who may also have established themselves on the eastern part of Cyprus? Or were they the consequence of internal conflicts among the various clans, as suggested by Catling (15) and Aström? The problem remains unsolved.

There must have been significant changes in the way of life, since, apart from important villages, towns such as Enkomi sprang into existence. The majority of the population continued to live a pastoral life, but the fields were cultivated more systematically and the mines were more intensively worked. The exportation of metal went hand in hand with the trade in pottery, some of which even reached Cilicia.

Art

The objects found in the tombs betray a mood of anxiety which was to end, as far as pottery is concerned, in a stylistic renewal. Having exhausted the possibilities of the polished red ware, the potter laid aside his engraving and polishing tools in favor of the brush. A similar transition was taking place in Crete and on the shores of Anatolia at about this time, and it is quite possible that the local craftsmen, caught in the wake of the new fashion, followed the foreign lead.

We have seen that white-painted ware had already appeared during the last phase of the Early Bronze Age. It now came into its own and its influence was to persist into the early sixteenth century. The rather dark decoration, in black, red or brown, stands out sharply against the buff of the clay walls or the whitish slip, slightly shiny at first, but mat later on. The linear motifs hug the contours of the vessel, enclosing it in a web of horizontal (pages 47, 54) or perpendicular (page 57) bands enlivened with lattice, herringbone and checkerboard designs. The spirit and the geometric conception are the same, but the brush strokes are more supple than the necessarily stiff, though lighter, strokes of the engraving point. Indeed, one is conscious of a certain heaviness in the treatment, accentuated by a sort of "horror of the void" (page 57). This suggests a possible psychological link with the dark and uneasy historical climate, which the craftsman may unconsciously have allowed to guide his hand.

During this period, the technique of working in bronze, which was acquiring ever greater importance, had obvious repercussions on ceramics. Two other kinds of pottery reveal the intention to substitute for metal a material which, while retaining the appearance of the prototype, was more malleable and, at the same time, cheaper. Thus, in addition to white-

HORNED GOD. Apollo Alasiotas? Keraetas?   *Solid bronze. Height: 54.2 cm.*

76   *Iron I (twelfth century B.C.).*   *Enkomi (Famagusta).*   *Cyprus Museum, Nicosia.*

STATUETTE OF A MAN SEATED ON A THRONE.
Bronze. Height: 14.5 cm.   *Iron I (twelfth century B.C.).*
Enkomi (Famagusta).   *Musée du Louvre, Paris.*

painted ware, various examples of black-slip ware and red-on-black ware have been found. It is clear from both the shape of the pots and their decoration, which is very restrained and in light linear relief, that the potter was trying to imitate metal models (page 66).

The trend toward moderation and greater austerity is equally apparent in the conception of the forms. The earlier baroque complexity and capricious flights of fancy are conspicuously absent. It is no longer a question of sheer elegance or gay and sprightly tricks. The vessels tend to draw in, to divest themselves of every superfluous element, except for the painted

SCEPTER WITH TWO FALCONS.   *Gold and cloisonné enamel. Height: 16.5 cm.*
(Eleventh century, ca. 1050 B.C.).   *Kourion.*   *Cyprus Museum, Nicosia.*

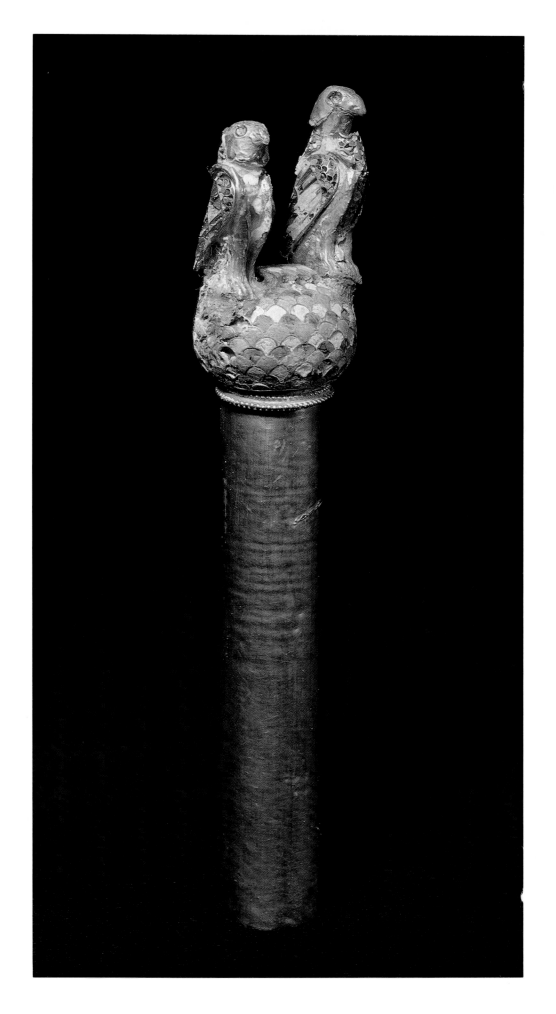

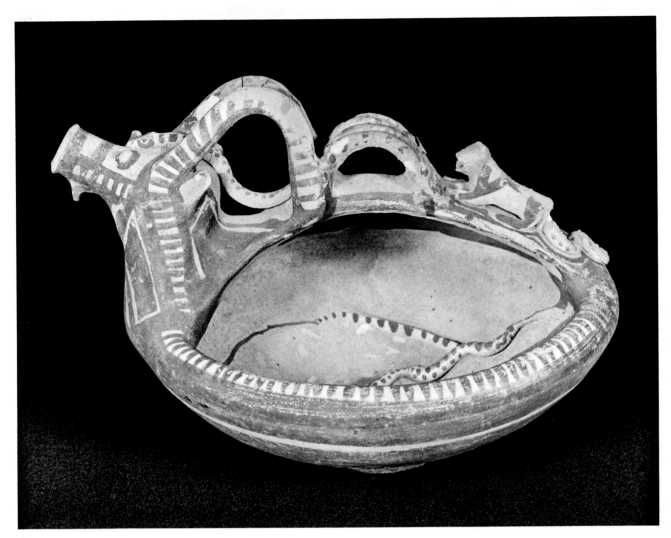

RING-SHAPED VASE.   *Molded decoration : serpent and animals. Terra-cotta. Diam.: 24 cm.*
Late Bronze III (1230–1050 B.C.).   *Cyprus Museum, Nicosia.*

decoration. There are pitchers with schematic and rudimentary figures of animals and men, timidly recalling the plastic invention of the Early Bronze Age, but they are rare.

Imagination and humor appear to have given place to a greater pragmatism, to the taste for efficient form, to technical progress.

Side by side with the classical pitchers, jugs, amphoras and bowls, sculptured vases in the form of animals, birds and even fish continued to be produced. Anthropomorphic ceramics (in which the vessel personifies man and a narrative theme is superimposed on the utilitarian function) grew more common (16). Thus, the neck of the vessel usually became a human head or the vase itself was metamorphosed into a fertility goddess, closely resembling the idols in form. This particular type of vessel, in which Cyprus excelled and whose origins are to be sought in the Orient and Northern Syria, was to be systematically produced during the Late Bronze Age.

CYLINDRICAL AMPHORA.   *Terra-cotta. Height: 35.7 cm.*
Cypro-Geometric I (1050–950 B.C.).   *Kourion.*   *Cyprus Museum, Nicosia.*

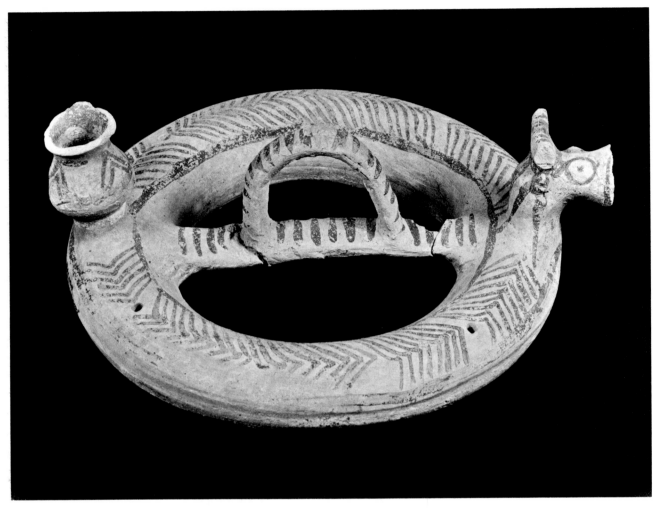

RING-SHAPED VASE.
Late Bronze III C (1100–1050 B.C.).

Terra-cotta. Proto-white-painted-ware. Width : 22.3 cm.
Cyprus Museum, Nicosia.

Idols

During this period the idols, which show evidence of a more studious treatment, underwent minor formal modifications. They continued in the flat tradition, but it is already possible to detect in the details (the heads, for example) the beginning of a return to carving in the round. Moreover, under the influence of current fashion, their makers adopted the white-slip form of decoration.

The reliefs of Karmi

The universal pressure for change is particularly apparent in the funerary architecture. The tombs became more elaborate and more luxurious. Probably inspired by the Egyptian mastabas, the architects adopted decoration in relief. Thus, the excavation of the necropolis of Karmi has revealed a funerary chamber whose lintel has been carved in a bas-relief representing the exterior of a house, while one of the walls of the dromos is decorated with a human figure. This is the only known evidence of an attempt at monumental sculpture on the part of the Cypriots of that period.

KALATHOS.   *Proto-white-painted-ware. Height : 15 cm, diam. : 27 cm.*
Late Bronze III C (1100–1050 B.C.).   *Kouklia.*   *Cyprus Museum, Nicosia.*

Objects in bronze

Growing prosperity is also indicated by the abundant finds of objects, tools and weapons in bronze. The mounting foreign demand must certainly have resulted in the establishment of foundries capable of operating on a more organized basis. From these small beginnings there later arose a to some extent industrialized form of metal-working, as illustrated by the workshops of Enkomi.

LATE BRONZE AGE OR LATE CYPRIOT (1600–1050 B.C.)

The historical context

During the Late Bronze Age Europe was caught in the throes of a great succession of migratory movements, which continued into the Iron Age.

Waves of warrior tribesmen from the Balkans and Illyria swept north and south, destroying all before them and leaving only ruins and despair in their path.

83

The eastern Mediterranean and the Aegean were the scene of vast conflicts in which states large and small became embroiled. Great power rivalry raged unrestrained, imperialistic ambitions were unleashed, war followed war, and the peoples were mercilessly harassed.

Having scattered the Hyksos in Palestine, Egypt saw the birth of the New Kingdom and the founding of the redoubtable eighteenth and nineteenth dynasties, whose Pharaohs – builders, warriors and conquerors – strengthened the royal autocracy, modified the forms of worship (reforms of Akhenaten), and for four centuries imposed their economic power, institutions and culture on the Near East.

Vast migrations took place under the growing pressure of the Indo-Europeans who had flooded into Iran. Lower Mesopotamia was occupied by Kassite hillmen (1595–1153). During the fifteenth century, the Hurrians, coming from Kurdistan, took Syria and Mesopotamia away from the Amorites and Hittites and reached Elam. Then, during the thirteenth and twelfth centuries, came the invasion of the controversial Sea Peoples, who, leaving a trail of fire and blood, uprooted the local populations, brought down the Hittite empire (about 1190) and attacked Egypt, which emerged from the struggle exhausted and ready to yield to the Lybian chiefs.

At the end of the twelfth century a new Semitic tribe, the Aramaeans, appeared. Establishing themselves on the west bank of the Jordan, the Aramaeans imposed their will on the Syrian cities (eleventh and tenth centuries) and for years roamed Assyria and Babylonia, pillaging as they went.

Thus, for three centuries, between about 1200 and 900 B.C., the eastern Mediterranean and the Near East were plagued with obscurantism, incertitude, and suffering.

Meanwhile, Greece and the Aegean were not spared. For four centuries (about 1525–1125 B.C.) the Mycenaeans reigned, extending their hegemony and their civilization throughout the Aegean and maintaining close relations with the Middle East and even the countries of central and northern Europe, from which they obtained amber. In about 1400 the kingdom of Minos crumbled beneath the blows of its conquerors; the Achaean allies embarked on their adventurous siege of Troy, which fell about 1240; and the Dorians overran the Peloponnesus (eleventh century?), destroyed the Mycenaean civilization and pursued the native populations toward the isles and the coasts of Anatolia.

But the inescapable destiny of conquered and conquerors is not exclusively controlled by baneful influences. This violent clash of civilizations, this continuous coming and going of invaders and refugees, this mingling of diverse cultures inevitably broadened the field of knowledge.

The major role played by contacts with the Aegean world in the cultural experience of Cyprus is further illustrated by the appearance about 1500 B.C. of syllabic writing, which remained in use until the beginning of the eleventh century. This writing, which seems to be related to the Cretan Linear A, was discovered (Enkomi, 1955) on an engraved clay tablet bearing a Cypro-Minoan text (17).

HORN-SHAPED VASE.
Cypro-Geometric I (1050–950 B.C.).

Terra-cotta. Length: 28 cm.
Cyprus Museum, Nicosia.

84

FIGURINE OF A DIVINITY.
Cypro-Geometric (tenth century B.C.).
Morphou Region.

Terra-cotta. Height: 16 cm.

Cyprus Museum, Nicosia.

The continuous fighting resulted in intensified exchanges among the peoples involved and hence the diffusion of new techniques. The invasion of the Sea Peoples and the migratory movements that spread through Europe in the centuries that followed were responsible for the dissemination of iron-smelting, which inaugurated a new era of economic evolution.

LARGE AMPHORA.
Cypro-Geometric III (850–700 B.C.).

Terra-cotta. Height: 61 cm.
Musée d'Art et d'Histoire, Geneva.

Cyprus during the Late Bronze Age

The Late Bronze Age was one of the most brilliant phases of Cypriot civilization. Inevitably, the upheavals in the Aegean and the Near East had their effect on the political and social structure of the island as well as on its culture and art.

Under this crossfire of violence and misery there were two events in particular that profoundly modified the face of civilization on Cyprus: the Pharaonic domination and the Hellenization of the island begun by the Mycenaeans (end of the fifteenth century) and completed by the Achaeans (end of the thirteenth and twelfth centuries).

In view of its geographical position and supplies of copper, an essential raw material for weapons of war, Cyprus could not escape involvement in the rivalries of the great powers. This is attested by historical documents reproduced in Egyptian and Mesopotamian texts. The hieroglyphic inscription that Rameses III, in celebration of his victories, had engraved on one of the pylons of the temple of Medinet Habu about 1196 B.C. cites, among the conquered territories, the kingdom of Asy or Alasia, which the majority of specialists agree in identifying with Cyprus.

Similarly, the tablets of Mari tell of the import of copper from Enkomi by way of Ugarit. Relations with Alasia, which reached their peak in the thirteenth century, are often mentioned in the archives of the last kings of that city. Between 1484 and 1464, Tuthmosis II, the most powerful Pharaoh of the eighteenth dynasty, subdued Syria, triumphed over the army of the Mitanni and probably made vassals of the Cypriots. Henceforth the rulers of Cyprus were to pay tribute to the great king and accept his peace and culture.

The occupation of Egypt by the Hyksos meant that the Egyptian navy no longer controlled the eastern Mediterranean, and this brought confusion to the sea routes that led along the Syrian coast. As a result, Cretan trade became more closely oriented toward the Aegean world. But the triumph of the eighteenth dynasty and the scattering of the occupiers restored the security of the trade routes, with dramatic consequences for the countries bordering the Aegean.

Mycenae, then at the height of its power, entered into rivalry with Crete, seized Knossos in about 1400 B.C. and took its place in foreign trade. Mycenaean products were soon to be found throughout the Middle East. Toward the end of the fifteenth century Mycenaean merchants established themselves on Cyprus. The prosperity of the cities of Enkomi, Kition and Kourion and their cosmopolitan character formed the attraction for the newcomers, whose aim was to dominate the commercial market.

The abundance of Mycenaean ceramics and jewelry discovered in the tombs and necropolises of the south and east of the island testifies to their active presence.

More trade and closer relations with neighboring countries led to an era of prosperity based on Cyprus's privileged geographical position, the intensive exploitation of its copper mines, and its growing commercial importance.

There is other evidence of the profound changes that must have taken place during this period. The local potentates, who had formerly ruled over modest communities or large

JAR RESTING ON TRIPOD.   *Terra-cotta. Height: 19 cm, diam.: 15 cm.*
Cypro-Geometric III (850–700 B.C.).   *Lefkoniko.*   *Cyprus Museum, Nicosia.*

HEAD OF A BROKEN STATUE.　　　　　　　*Terra-cotta. Height: 20.5 cm.*
Cypro-Geometric (eighth century B.C.) or Cypro-Archaic I (seventh century B.C.).
Fletcher Fund, 1935.　　　　　　　　　　*Metropolitan Museum, New York.*

villages, became kings who built cities, within whose fortified walls the population could go about its peaceful tasks in perfect security.

Enkomi

It is Enkomi that offers the best glimpse of the Cypriot civilization of those days. The first clues to its existence undoubtedly date from the beginning of the Middle Bronze Age (2000–1700). At that time, however, it was little more than a village (the most important center on

HORSEMAN.　　　　　　　　　　　　*Terra-cotta. Height: 21 cm.*
Cypro-Archaic I (700–600 B.C.)?　　　　*Cyprus Museum, Nicosia.*

the island was then Kalopsidha in the Famagusta district), which appears to have been destroyed about 1750. This would correspond to the passage of the Hyksos, who may have established themselves in the eastern part of the island, and would explain why so few of the finds at Enkomi relate to the seventeenth or the early sixteenth century. The revival of Enkomi dates from about 1550, when it began gradually to develop into the most active and important town on the island, remaining to all intents and purposes its capital for two centuries and a half.

The excavations of the various missions (1896, British Mission; 1927–30, Swedish Expedition; 1934–38, Professor Cl. F. A. Schaeffer; 1948–56, D.A.C. in collaboration with Professor Cl. F. A. Schaeffer) have been very revealing. They have disclosed an extensive city covering a necropolis. The fact that the sea has since receded almost two miles has considerably modified the topographical aspect of the site, which was originally situated on the coast. An important harbor and trading center, the city was a convenient port of call for ships heading for Anatolia or the Aegean. Toward the thirteenth century, threatened from abroad, the cautious monarch had the city surrounded by a huge Cyclopean stone wall, along whose ramparts he erected a string of watchtowers overlooking the Mesaoria plain and the sea.

The city occupied an approximately square site about 440 yards long and 385 yards across. The streets, which intersect at right angles, were ten feet wide and bordered by large and luxurious houses, some in the Mycenaean megaron style, built of big blocks of hewn stone. The important public buildings were erected around a central paved square. Two sanctuaries of some consequence have also been excavated, together with bronze foundries which attest the importance that the art of metal-working had acquired by that time.

But an inexorable fate was in store for the city. Like many other places on Cyprus, and in Anatolia and Egypt, Enkomi was not to be spared the plague of the Sea Peoples. Their passage was marked by a trail of destruction and carnage. About 1075, as the city was nursing its wounds as best it could, it received the *coup de grâce*, a violent earthquake that reduced it to rubble.

Its inhabitants, fleeing this scene of desolation, took refuge in the future Salamis, the legendary city founded by Teucer, brother of Ajax, on his return from Troy. According to another version, the silting up of the harbor also contributed to the abandonment of the city.

The wealth, taste, cultural level and well-being of the inhabitants of Enkomi are expressed in the remarkable grave goods discovered in the tombs, in the high quality of the works of art, such as the solid bronze statue of the Horned God found in one of the sanctuaries (page 77), and in the variety and refinement of the ceramics.

Much of their progress was undoubtedly due to close contact with countries at an advanced level of civilization, from whom the Cypriots learned many valuable lessons.

Mycenaean influence was especially widespread, being expressed in stylistic changes in ceramics, modifications in architecture, new religious customs, and technical developments.

CHARIOT WITH TWO HORSES AND THREE WARRIORS. Terra-cotta. Height: 16.5 cm. Cypro-Archaic I (700–600 B.C.). Ovgoros "Schionia" (Famagusta). Cyprus Museum, Nicosia.

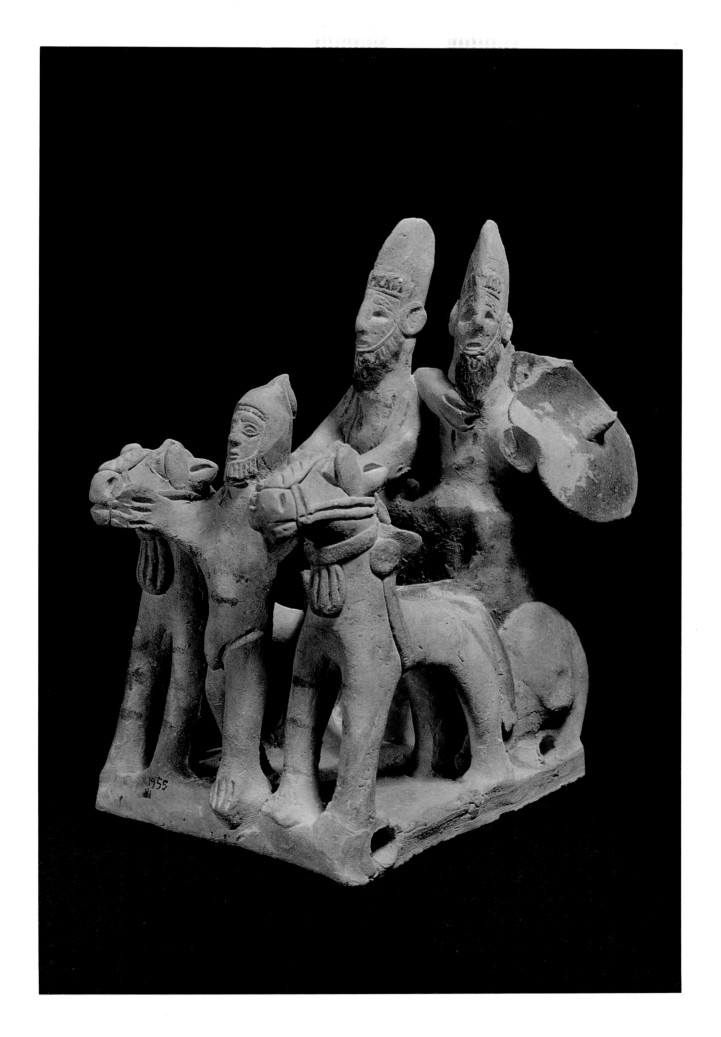

FIGURE WITH A SMALLER FIGURE IN HIS ARMS.
Terra-cotta. Height : 12 cm.   *Cypro-Archaic I (700–600 B.C.)?*
Episcopi (Limassol).   *Cyprus Museum, Nicosia.*

However, the part played by neighbors to the east was no less conspicuous. Thus one can trace cultural analogies between Cyprus and Ras Shamra, where, according to Professor Schaeffer, there were Cypriot and Aegean colonies.

The artistic contribution
The outcome is particularly apparent in the domain of the arts, which is crisscrossed by new trends and influences, ideas in gestation, progressive urges, and nostalgia for the past.

Continual conflict reflected the strains in the structure of a society whose foundations were still shaky and uncertain, a society seeking the stability that it was only to find in absorption

MALE STATUETTE.
Terra-cotta.   Height : 35 cm.
Cypro-Archaic I (700–600 B.C.).
Cyprus Museum, Nicosia.

95

into the Greek world. Blunted by contradictory aspirations, the advance toward a new form of civilization took shape as a slow and hesitant process of adaptation.

The Cypriot, proud and independent, strove to retain the special cachet that distinguished his work from that of his neighbor and master. Accordingly, he proceeded by selection. Among the elements offered by Western rationalism and the sensual East he chose those that appealed to his taste, spicing them with his own inventiveness and imaginative force and with his bent for decoration rich in capricious motifs, modifying and creating forms.

Pottery

At the beginning of the Late Bronze Age the influence of metallurgy, which was to continue to be felt until the end of the thirteenth century, became even more apparent. The potter increasingly followed the example of the worker in bronze (page 66). Alongside the traditional forms other variants appeared, for example, the wide-mouthed pitcher with pinched lips that seems to have been derived from Syrian or Cilician models (page 65). As for the colors, they were restricted to those that simulated the appearance of metal, with a dark luster pleasant to the touch. The decoration of the surfaces was austere and in low relief, either smooth or hatched. The vessels are of the base-ring type made on Cyprus between 1600 and 1200 B.C. Similar pottery has been found in Syria, Palestine and Egypt.

Technical advances brought an improvement in quality and finish. The potters were now using the wheel, which enabled them to create forms less individual but more refined and more harmonious in their proportions. The mechanization of the craft also placed restraints on the imagination. Long spouts and excrescences were not appropriate to wheel-thrown forms. This did not prevent the hemispherical bowls and white-slip ware with its geometric decoration – black and brown ladders and checkerboard squares – from being highly prized not only in Egypt and Syria but also in the Archipelago, at Thera, Melos, in Attica and at Hissarlik (Troy).

Intensive trading presupposes a highly developed merchant marine, which the Cypriots did not possess. Thus it was the Aegeans who, profiting from the prosperity of the island, served as intermediaries between producers and consumers.

Mycenaean period

The penetration of Mycenaean elements, starting in the early fourteenth century, led to profound changes in the creative spirit of the island's artists. Within a century the culture and the art of the new arrivals had been accepted and were contributing to the formation of a local school.

Actually, the factors responsible for cultural unity, already apparent in the sixteenth century in the archipelago dominated by the Mycenaeans, did not operate on Cyprus, whose historical past and culture were firmly in the orbit of the Middle East. The presence on the island of large quantities of Mycenaean pottery has stirred controversy and raises the question

FEMALE STATUETTE.
Cypro-Archaic I (700–600 B.C.).   *Arsos (Larnaca).*   *Terra-cotta. Height: 33 cm, width: 12 cm.*   *Cyprus Museum, Nicosia.*

BOAT WITH THREE FIGURES.   *Terra-cotta. Height: 16 cm, length: 30 cm.*
Cypro-Archaic I (700–600 B.C.).   *Kalochorio tis Klirou (Nicosia).*   *Cyprus Museum, Nicosia.*

of the possible existence of local workshops (18). In fact, more Mycenaean vessels have been found on Cyprus than anywhere else within the Mycenaean sphere of influence, and some of them exhibit very diverse characteristics, such as the "pictorial style" in decoration or the adoption of local or oriental forms. Faced with these alternatives, there are specialists who maintain that all the pottery in this specific style, found not only on the island but also at Troy, along the Syrian and Palestinian coasts and as far away as Egypt, was produced in the Peloponnesus. If there are details that distinguish these products from those of Mycenae, they are, it is said, no more than unavoidable concessions to the taste of a potential new market.

Other archeologists refuse to accept this explanation. On the contrary, they believe that after 1400 B.C. Mycenaean artisans accompanying the merchants established themselves in the trading centers of Enkomi, Kition and Kourion and created the so-called Cypro-Mycenaean style, which employs traditional Aegean forms but also draws inspiration from the local repertory (bowls with ogival handles, base-ring and white-slip pitchers [page 73], lentiform gourds, etc.). Regardless of the scientific controversy, the existence of a local style

HORSES AND RIDER.   *Terra-cotta. Height: 22.5 cm.*
Cypro-Archaic I (700–600 B.C.).   *Cyprus Museum, Nicosia.*

is incontestable. The exigencies of this style are of more than functional significance, they represent a reaction against servile imitation, an expression of independence from imposed prototypes, and a need for renewal.

Since the beginning of the fourteenth century the Mycenaean pottery of Cyprus had included a considerable proportion of large amphora-like or wide-mouthed kraters whose origin can be traced to metal models. Other types continued in use or were adapted from Aegean or Oriental prototypes according to the fancy of the local artist and their intended function, religious or profane. Elegantly stemmed goblets, smooth bowls, rhytons, kylikes, and urns, were among the many products of the Mycenaean period.

Although, all in all, the repertory of forms was rather limited, the decoration displayed considerable variety, not so much in the somewhat standardized subject matter, probably dictated by the customer, which is confined to certain motifs in the Mycenaean bestiary or chariot decoration, but in the freedom of the drawing, a certain ornamental fantasy, and a greater exuberance.

It is interesting and rather easy to trace the evolutionary curve of preferred forms and motifs from one period to another, together with the changes in decoration. As I have already mentioned, at the beginning of the fourteenth century the amphoroidal and wide-mouthed kraters were the types of vessels most appreciated. In fact, they were particularly well suited to the preoccupations of the moment, being better adapted to the pictorial than the ornamental style. The decoration took its cue from fresco painting of the type to be found in restored Knossos, which explains the title "palace style" (toward the middle of the fifteenth century).

A fine example of this painting is afforded by an amphora from the beginning of the fourteenth century (page 73) in which the pictorial tendency, common to all the Mycenaean pottery of Cyprus, is obvious. The drawing and composition are in the Aegean tradition, but the decorative exuberance and the sense of color are strictly Oriental.

According to Nilsson, whose interpretation seems the most convincing of the several that have been offered, the scene depicts an episode from the Iliad in which Zeus holds the scales of destiny before the chariot driven by the heroes as they speed into battle. The motifs (octopus, chariot, human figures, flying birds, horses) are strewn with a generous hand over the belly of the vessel and projected on the two-dimensional screen of the ground without overcrowding but, at the same time, without concern for the notion of real space. The chromatic play of the gleaming brown surfaces, flecked with white, and the contrasting lines and dots is vibrant and dynamic, and the movement it suggests is further accentuated by the schematic drawing.

It is well known that what characterizes the pottery of the Mycenaean III is the choice of motifs inspired by nature, leading, though in isolated cases only, to the faithful reproduction of reality. Here, all is simplified, schematized, for stylization serves to accentuate the decorative effect. But as soon as the disciplined line begins to play a preponderant role, the potter can

ASKOS.
Cypro-Archaic I (700–600 B.C.).

Terra-cotta. Height: 25 cm, width: 14 cm.
Cyprus Museum, Nicosia.

100

STEMMED BOWL.   *Terra-cotta. Height: 16.2 cm, diam.: 18 cm.*
Cypro-Archaic I (700–600 B.C.).   *Larnaca District.*   *Cyprus Museum, Nicosia.*

make free use of linear motifs to divide the surface into horizontal zones. Thus the eye is flattered by the balance and harmonious rhythm of the alternation of ornamented areas and patches of bare ground in pale monochrome, where only the sensuality of the material is retained.

The operation of kilns at oxidizing temperatures made polychromy impracticable, since the colors were spoiled in the firing process. That is why most of the vessels were reduced, decoratively speaking, simply to a dark design on a white ground. The preferred motif of this style (Mycenaean III A), especially during the first half of the fourteenth century, was the chariot, usually manned by two men. Auxiliary elements served to fill in the background. At

LARGE AMPHORA.   *Terra-cotta. Height: 81 cm, diam. of opening: 36.4 cm.*
Cypro-Archaic I (700–600 B.C.).   *Trikomo (Famagusta).*   *Cyprus Museum, Nicosia.*

first, these were trees or rocky landscape rendered in a fairly realistic, evocative style. But in the course of time these supplementary motifs multiplied, becoming stylized and eventually, toward the end of the fourteenth century, purely decorative (Amarna style, 1375–1350 B.C.).

The other motifs in vogue during the Mycenaean III A were bulls, processions of armed men, and rhythmic friezes of birds or animals, somewhat Oriental in inspiration.

The pictorial style continued its glorious career through the thirteenth century, but after the almost total disappearance of the "palace style" some significant changes took place.

The period that followed (Mycenaean III B) saw the previous forms give way to the bell krater with horizontal handles. On the other hand, as the decoration was further simplified, the ceramist was able to make use of other typical forms, such as the urn or the broad shallow bowl, which despite its increased width, preserved a distinctive elegance and lent itself admirably to ornamentation in circular bands.

The spirit of the decoration now swung toward realism, and the schematization that had inevitably led to a certain angularization of the forms was transmuted into undulations and curves. Since the available length of the decorated zone had increased, the painter deformed and elongated the bodies of his animals, abjured naturalistic servility, and took up the purely esthetic option. The drawing is skilful, studied, more precise and more personal (19). The chariot motif has disappeared in favor of peaceful scenes in which confrontations of animals, birds, fish or combinations of these creatures predominate. Every superfluous element has been eliminated. There remains only the principal theme whose primacy is affirmed against the empty background of the pale clay. These remarks are well illustrated in the krater (end of thirteenth century, page 71) found at Enkomi, the last great work of the Cypro-Mycenaean school before it entered its period of decadence.

No craft is immune to external influence. Thus, we have already noted that metal-working had modified the forms and decoration employed by the potters.

During the Mycenaean III B the use of luxury fabrics, tapestries and ivories imported from the Near East began to be reflected in the ceramics. Bands of animals, bulls, for example, may be found pleasingly disposed among broad fields full of different ornamental motifs (crosses, circles, dots, etc.). The eye wanders easily over these friezes in which half-tones alternate agreeably with patches of dark and light. Once caught up in the rhythm of the undulating contour, we from time to time encounter certain unexpected checks, little surprises that create a delightfully melodic effect. The use of this language, which gave the demiurge a chance to exploit his gifts of imagination in complete freedom, reaffirms the originality of Cypriot art. The comparison with the austere restraint of Mycenaean work is convincing in this respect.

Toward the end of the thirteenth century embroidered cloth and tapestries lost their ascendancy and the succeeding style was more influenced by engraving, particularly on ivory but also on wood and stone (20).

OENOCHOË.
104   *Cypro-Archaic I (700–600 B.C.).*   *Terra-cotta. Height: 38.1 cm, width: 28.6 cm.*
                                                         Cyprus Museum, Nicosia.

WARRIOR BEARING A SHIELD. *Terra-cotta. Height: 17.3 cm.*
Cypro-Archaic I (700–600 B.C.). *Cyprus Museum, Nicosia.*

This style was characterized by an incisive stroke that attempted to render plasticity by varying the thickness of the line. Whereas formerly the artist had been primarily concerned with the decorative effect, he was now obliged to rely exclusively on the drawing, on the skill and steadiness of his hand, on training and keen observation.

The adoption of this new graphic technique opened the way to a greater realism, to a more "classical" and less "archaic" conception. This is apparent in the effort made to portray various anatomical details (the veins of the leg, the muzzle, etc.) with greater precision. But

PITCHER.
Cypro-Archaic I (700–600 B.C.).

Terra-cotta. Height: 16.5 cm.
Cyprus Museum, Nicosia.

the artist was not content to stop there. He tried to recreate the sensation of volume, in exclusively plastic terms, by using the curved line to suggest a third dimension (page 71). This was a step of special importance, since it represented the first attempt in Greek art to express a more precise realism.

Toward the end of the century, however, probably after the island had suffered some tragic blow, the treatment became heavier and more academic, the forms more angular, the quality of the paste less fine, the drawing wearier and less spontaneous. The pictorial style, which for two centuries had shone so brilliantly, was sinking into an inglorious twilight.

The Achaean colonization and final Hellenization of the island

Halfway through the second millennium Cyprus was already being infiltrated by small groups of Achaeans, but their presence did not really begin to be felt until after the destruction of the Mycenaean cities about the end of the thirteenth century. The colonization and final Hellenization of the island took place a century later.

The memory of this migration, which involved Rhodes, Cyprus, and part of the southern coast of Asia Minor, is perpetuated in classical legend and literature which give the names of the Greek heroes who after the fall of Troy (about 1200) came to Cyprus to rebuild the cities (Enkomi, Kition) or found new ones. Thus, according to tradition, the founder of Salamis was Teucer, brother of Ajax; Agapenor, king of Tegea in Arcadia, is supposed to have founded Paphos, Praxander Lapithos, and Akamas and his brother Demophon, sons of Theseus, king of Athens, Soloi, whereas Idalion claims to have been founded by Chalcanor. Moreover, the presence of the Achaeans is attested by numerous archeological finds made in various parts of Cyprus.

The Achaean colonization was important in that it implied the almost total disappearance of the long Oriental tradition. It toppled all the ancient structures and, adding to the already considerable contribution of the Mycenaeans, gave the civilization of the island the final push needed to carry it irreversibly into the orbit of the Hellenic world.

The Achaeans, a tenacious people with an advanced culture, imposed their will peacefully on the native population, whom they dominated but did not enslave.

Apart from improved building methods and new styles of urban, religious and funerary architecture, they introduced their language and writing, their institutions, their customs and usages, and their religion.

Though less important than the Mycenaean influence, the artistic contribution of the Achaeans gave a new stimulus to the native arts.

KRATER.
Cypro-Archaic I (700–600 B.C.).

Terra-cotta. Height: 45.5 cm.
Cyprus Museum, Nicosia.

PITCHER.   Terra-cotta. Height: 24 cm. Free-field style.
Cypro-Archaic I (700–600 B.C.).   Cyprus Museum, Nicosia.

Pottery

Their arrival coincided with the introduction of a new and austere style of pottery from Argolis (Mycenaean III C 1). Rather limited in expression, its principal characteristic is the spiral motif and a lack of themes drawn from the earlier repertoire. Scarcely any use is made of motifs involving birds and fishes. This pottery was quickly accepted and gradually superseded everything that had gone before. At Enkomi and Kition it enjoyed an almost total monopoly, which implies that the new colonists had succeeded in imposing their particular personal tastes.

In the course of the first half of the eleventh century the Cypriot artists developed a style of their own in ceramics known as "proto-white painted ware." It displays little in the way of

PITCHER.   *Terra-cotta. Height: 22.5 cm. Free-field style.*
Cypro-Archaic I (700–600 B.C.).
Petrakides Collection, Larnaca.   *Cyprus Museum, Nicosia.*

new invention. The forms and decoration are clearly inspired by the "granary style" of the Mycenaeans. But even in this case there has been an intrusion of other motifs of local or Oriental origin. This pottery is regarded as an intermediate link between the Mycenaean pictorial style and the style of the Iron Age.

The decoration is conventional and not particularly well conceived, more the work of an artisan than an artist. The former springs of the imagination have run dry and technique has killed inspiration.

The ornamentation is strictly geometric and linear, dividing the vessels into horizontal bands. These bands are decorated with a great variety of motifs: chevrons, wavy lines forming closed circles, checkerboards, triangles arranged in squares, alternating with compact zones in dull black or areas of white. The effect thus created is rather special, a little clumsy, commonplace, austere and lacking in resonance. The only exception is a bichrome kalathos whose geometric decoration, probably of Syrian origin, includes palms, swastikas, birds, human figures, union jacks, etc. All this has the effect of breaking the monotony and suggests the existence of a less commercialized product aimed at a more discerning public. The most popular forms were small and large amphoras, pitchers and bowls; less common were lentiform gourds, duck-shaped askos, bottles, and a kernos. A great deal of material of this type was found in 1966 in a tomb at Kouklia (Palaepaphos) (21), the similarities of form and decoration being striking as compared with other finds (Kaloriziki, Lapithos, Idalion, Salamis) (22).

Jewelry

The finds at Enkomi and Kition are matched only by the treasures of the royal tombs of Mycenae. The incomparable gold jewelry includes diadems embossed with volutes, rosettes, lotus flowers, and ram's heads; pomegranate pendants of exquisite workmanship; earrings in the form of teardrops and bull's heads; beaded and twisted collars and necklaces; repoussé breastplates; and rings chased by master goldsmiths.

Particularly noteworthy is the extraordinary discovery of a gold scepter (page 79) in a tomb, probably royal, of the Kaloriziki necropolis at Kourion, a city colonized, according to Herodotus, by the Argives.

This admirable find consists of a tube of gold ending in a sphere encrusted with enamels on which two falcons are daintily perched.

The workmanship is evidence of a highly advanced technique which the specialists initially attributed to a very late period (Byzantine and then Archaic). However, when the tomb was re-excavated by the expedition mounted by the Pennsylvania University Museum, it was shown to date from the eleventh century.

Professor Schaeffer has also discovered in a fourteenth-century tomb a magnificent silver bowl decorated with bucrania and highly stylized, incrusted flowers of unusual beauty.

Most of these jewels are in a style that can withstand any comparison. They are examples of that genuinely Cypriot taste for juggling with heterogeneous, Oriental and Aegean, elements to arrive at results full of imagination and unexpected subtlety. Thus, certain thirteenth- and fourteenth-century diadems of Oriental inspiration are decorated with spirals, sphynxes, lions, and shells borrowed from the cycle of "Aegean art."

According to V. Karageorghis, these objects were not imported. More probably, they were the products of Mycenaean craftsmen already established on the island who passed on to the natives their knowledge and style, for the mere sight of the prototypes could scarcely have had such a profound influence on the work of the Cypriot goldsmith, heir, as he was, to so strong a local tradition (23).

KRATER WITH HIGH STEM.
Cypro-Archaic I (700–600 B.C.).

Terra-cotta. Bichrome redware. Height: 58 cm.
Cyprus Museum, Nicosia.

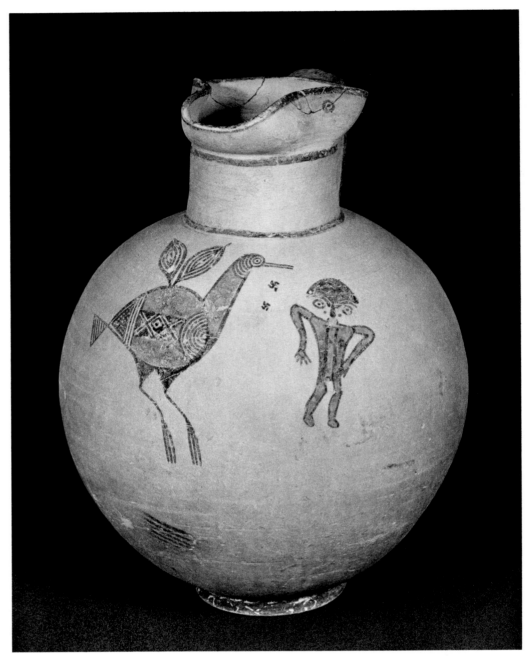

PITCHER.   *Terra-cotta. Height : 33.8 cm. Free-field style.*
Cypro-Archaic I (700–600 B.C.).   *Cyprus Museum, Nicosia.*

It would take too long to describe in detail the numerous and varied products of the so-called minor arts, evidence of the splendor of a civilization now approaching its apogee. But how can one omit to mention those finely carved ivories, such as the superb, delicately incised mirror frame found at Kouklia, showing a warrior in heroic combat with a lion, or the cylinders illustrating devotional practices and everyday occupations. Here, too, we observe that interpenetration of styles and techniques, that multiplicity of influences that the Cypriot artist knew so well how to turn to advantage.

AMPHORA.   *Terra-cotta. Height : 35.6 cm.*
Cypro-Archaic I (700–600 B.C.).   *Cyprus Museum, Nicosia.*

The high quality of the finds is well maintained in the alabaster vases and perfume jars, whether made locally or imported, and in the faience ware, such as the magnificent conical rhyton of Kition (page 75). The blue glow of the enamel, the nielloed decoration with the black and red fillets that underline the chromatic values of the narrow fields, and the taste for realism and movement make this one of the masterpieces of so-called Aegeo-Oriental art.

Objects in bronze

The objects in bronze are no less important. It has been suggested that during the fourteenth and thirteenth centuries Cyprus failed to advance beyond the first stage of metallurgical research and that a genuine bronze industry did not develop until after the Achaean colonization. This seems a rather doubtful hypothesis. If the tombs have yielded little in the way of bronze dating from that period (1400–1200 B.C.), it must be because the custom of burying metal objects with the dead had been abolished. It is inconceivable that an island so rich in copper, so inventive and creative in related areas, should have awaited the arrival of the Mycenaeans to develop a craft for which the raw material was so readily available (24). Forgetting for the moment the statuary, which will be examined separately in the chapter devoted to sculpture, one need do no more than consider the objects of everyday use, the weapons – knives, swords and willow-leaf daggers – and the various forms of tripods cunningly decorated with friezes of hunting scenes, animal figures and geometric motifs. The style of the reliefs, careful and well-studied, often recalls the ivory work dear to the Aegeans, translated into the rougher idiom of the skilful local craftsmen.

The final phase (1150–1050 B.C.)

The Bronze Age ended on a dramatic note. The destruction of the Mycenaean cities by the Dorians brought to the island a new wave of Achaeans driven from their homeland. The Trojan war, typical of that troubled era, earthquakes, the invasion of the Sea Peoples were other brush strokes in the somber picture of life on Cyprus during those evil days.

Objects of art

The works of art produced during this period of transition were essentially pedestrian, even decadent, with esthetic considerations subordinated to technique, commercial products adapted to the prevailing mood. Except for certain parts of the sculptured vessels (page 80), which required the active intervention of the artist, almost all the pottery was turned on the wheel. The "Bucchero" type made its appearance. This vessel, intended to look like metal, dark-colored, monochrome and soberly decorated with simple spirals or vertical folds, was to remain popular during the following century.

PITCHER.
Cypro-Archaic I (700–600 B.C.).   *Arnadhi*   *Terra-cotta. Height: 28 cm. Free-field style.*
Cyprus Museum, Nicosia.

KEG JAR.
Cypro-Archaic I (700–600 B.C.).

Terra-cotta. Height: 39 cm.
Cyprus Museum, Nicosia.

The proto-white-painted style was also successfully continued, with the application of geometric decorative elements (pages 81, 82) and a quite Oriental exuberance of motifs (pages 81–83). The drawing, however, remains confined to repetition. Having lost its vigor and spontaneity it has grown clumsy and overloaded. The artist, no longer addressing a refined audience, is doing no more than required to satisfy the grosser needs of a less discriminating public.

PITCHER.
Cypro-Archaic I (700–600 B.C.).

Terra-cotta. Height: 23 cm. Free-field style.
Cyprus Museum, Nicosia.

THE IRON AGE

A technical revolution

For as long as their military and cultural power could withstand the pressure, the Mycenaeans were able to assimilate the invaders, and their strength only increased. But dark days lay ahead. The warlike Dorians, descendants of Herakles, arrived to claim the throne of their ancestor, in accordance with the legend, and laid waste everything in their path. This marked the end of the Bronze Age and the beginning of a new era.

The Oriental and Aegean cultures, which were based exclusively on bronze, discovered that iron also existed in large quantities and, moreover, was cheaper to refine and easier to work. This astonishing discovery was gradually to transform the economy.

Metallurgy is a complicated art that was originally mastered only after a long process of trial and error. Iron had been known to the Oriental civilizations, from Egypt to Mesopotamia and as far as the Indus, since the sixth millennium (25), but it had long remained as precious as gold, since for lack of more sophisticated techniques it could only be worked by cold hammering.

In the third millennium the Egyptians and Anatolians were already capable of working the metal hot, but the "soft" iron they obtained soon lost its hardness and cutting edge. It could be used only for such strictly limited purposes as fabricating models of weapons and implements or fashioning simple jewelry.

Roughly fifteen centuries were to pass before man succeeded in developing his range of tools and learning the technique of steelmaking, that is, how to introduce carbon into the metal and thus obtain an infinitely tougher product. In Cilicia, where this process was discovered at the beginning of the fourteenth century B.C., the secret was guarded jealously for two centuries by the Hittite rulers, who made it one of the cornerstones of their power and hegemony.

Since the beginning of the Mycenaean period iron had also been known to the Greeks. But the advance of the Sea Peoples, as they overran country after country, uprooting the local populations, scattered the early ironmakers all over the Orient, and with them their skills.

In the following centuries familiarity with the new metal spread through Europe, largely as a result of successive waves of migration.

Historical factors contributed to the development and universal diffusion of the new technology. Henceforth, starting from the first millennium, it was to play a vital part in material progress and the building of new cultures.

It should not be forgotten, however, that whereas weapons and tools come to be made almost exclusively of iron, bronze remained the preferred material of the artists, who cherished its nobility and handsome appearance.

PITCHER.
Cypro-Archaic I (700–600 B.C.).

Terra-cotta. Height: 23.4 cm. Free-field style.
Cyprus Museum, Nicosia.

PITCHER.   *Terra-cotta. Height: 32 cm, width: 26.5 cm. Free-field style.*
Cypro-Archaic I (700–600 B.C.).
Lefkoniko (Famagusta).   *Cyprus Museum, Nicosia.*

The historical context

The most striking aspect of this period, which led along winding and adventurous paths to the threshold of the Classical era, was the weakening and gradual decline of the powers that had for centuries dominated the Middle East. The relentless struggle in which they had engaged, the long series of alternating victories and defeats, had left them exhausted and easy prey for the armies of the Aramaeans and Indo-Europeans that were soon to fall upon

them. Three centuries of invasions and attacks by nomadic tribes completed the demoralization of the local populations.

After this ordeal, in the eleventh century only the Assyrians remained lords and masters in their own land, still eager for foreign conquest and still possessed of an army equal to their ambitions. Having subdued Mesopotamia and Syria, their kings relentlessly consolidated their power, not even hesitating to sack the holy city of Babylon (689). There followed the Egyptian campaigns, the pillage of Thebes (663) and Susa (about 640), episodes inscribed in Assyrian history in letters of fire. But the Medes and Babylonians had their revenge. After five years of warfare (614–609), the Persians succumbed beneath the blows of the coalition. Nineveh was taken in 612.

The Chaldaean dynasty was then in power in Babylon and the New Empire, under king Nebuchadnezzar (605–562), was experiencing its last days of splendor and magnificence.

For almost a century (1020–930) the Hebrew kingdom of Palestine enjoyed national unity. The glorious reigns of Saul (1020–1010), David (1010–970) and Solomon (970–930) illumined those troubled times, but the unity of the country did not survive the last of those three great kings. The land was divided between the usurper Jeroboam I, founder of Israel, and Rehoboam, who proclaimed himself king of Judah. Syria was cut into pieces. The Aramaeans, regrouped under the king of Damascus, occupied the interior of the country. The coastal regions fell easy prey to the Neo-Hittites and the Phoenicians. The former established themselves in the north, the latter in the center. Phoenicia was at that time (tenth century) at the height of its power. Masters of the port-kingdoms at the end of the caravan routes from Western Asia, astute traders cultivating good relations with the Israelites, in order to protect their commerce with Arabia, and profiting from the decline of Egyptian and Aegean rivals, the Phoenicians were ready to conquer the world. Toward 800 B.C. we find them in Cyprus (Kition). In the last third of the century, venturing further and further from the Ionian shores, they occupied key positions in the central Mediterranean. In about 730 they founded Carthage and began to visit the ports of Tuscany. Bold mariners, by the middle of the seventh century they had penetrated the Strait of Gibraltar and were loading cargoes of Spanish metal at Tartessos.

The Greek world was also changing and growing. From the "Dark Ages" (twelfth to ninth centuries) that succeeded the brilliant Mycenaean epic, there arose a new civilization without writing. The Archaic epoch, one of the most remakable in the history of the Hellenes, was tinted with the colors of the Orient. This heritage was to enrich its technology, its religion and its myths.

Invasions and the displacement of populations brought the Greeks to the shores of Asia. During the first millennium, from the Hellespont to Lycia, a whole string of cities, some famous, others more humble, sheltered the activities of an industrious and creative society. Their protected harbors offered secure berths for naval vessels and merchant ships alike. The land bridge to the east facilitated international trade. Soon their fleets were in undisputed

JAR ON TRIPOD.
Cypro-Archaic I (700–600 B.C.).

Terra-cotta. Height: 16 cm. Free-field style.
Cyprus Museum, Nicosia.

124

PITCHER. *Terra-cotta. Height : 25 cm. Free-field style.*
Cypro-Archaic I (700–600 B.C.). Lefkoniko (Famagusta). Cyprus Museum, Nicosia.

control of the great sea routes of the Mediterranean. Centers of learning and culture developed and Anatolia was quick to accept the Hellenic influence. During the seventh century the Greeks began to infiltrate the West. The shores of the Gulf of Taranto, Sicily and western Italy were soon dotted with Greek cities. In about 600 the Phocians founded Marseilles.

During the Archaic period the arts and letters flourished and the cultural foundations of Western civilization were laid.

From the empiricism of the Orient, from the confusion of concrete experiences, the Greeks isolated the idea, passing on to disinterested knowledge and the dignity of pure thought. It was this search for truth that brought them to the notion of beauty. In their language truth and beauty are synonymous.

PITCHER.   *Terra-cotta. Height : 29 cm. Free-field style.*
Cypro-Archaic I (700–600 B.C.).   Arnoudi.   Cyprus Museum, Nicosia.

CYPRUS DURING THE GEOMETRIC PERIOD (1050-700 B.C.)

The division of history into artificial slices of time, though convenient, is quite unrealistic.
Historical upheavals rarely produce a clean break in the evolution of a civilization stiffened
by a traditional past of conventions, survivals and borrowings.

As we have already seen, on Cyprus the transition from the Bronze Age to the period
that followed was not abrupt; there was no sudden turnabout or cultural discontinuity.
Indeed, the immediate impression is one of a certain homogeneity, a unity whose
origins are to be sought in a fusion of local elements, Aegeo-Cypriot and Mycenaean,
with others of Syro-Anatolian origin. Forced into the same mold, the rough edges   127

disappeared and the contrasts merged, though without becoming less evident or losing their individuality.

The upheavals that marked the end to the Bronze Age resulted in the interruption of communications with the Orient, but also a reappraisal that eventually led to an intensified exploitation of local possibilities.

Although the obscurity of the first two centuries has prompted some historians to refer to them as the "Cypriot Middle Ages," when the island reemerged into the light it was bustling with activity.

For about three centuries (from the beginning of the tenth to the end of the eighth), Cyprus prospered and profited from its independence. To further improve its trading position it sought a base on the Syrian coast, founding Posideon, a port of transit through which merchandise flowed to and from the Orient. About 742, after the destruction of the Phoenician cities by the Assyrians, the Cypriots, with their most troublesome competitors out of the way, were free to develop their seafaring and trading talents to the full. At this time, according to the ancient historians, the island was at the height of its maritime power, a "thalassocracy" that endured until the Assyrian conquest of 709 B.C.

The evidence of the stele found at Kition indicates that in those days Cyprus was politically well organized. There were nine city-states, of Greek origin to judge from the names of their sovereigns (Aegisthus of Idalion, Eteander of Paphos, Admitus of Tamissos, Onassagoras of Ledra, etc.). Following forms of organization whose prototypes are to be found in Homeric society, the monarch took upon himself the functions of overlord and high priest, imposing his laws and surrounding himself with a numerous and luxurious court.

Repositories of tradition, holders of power and wealth, grouped in cities supplied by the toilers in the surrounding countryside, the ruling classes managed the commerce and industry, organized the social life, and encouraged technical improvements and innovations.

The many finds from this period, including those at Salamis, starting from the eleventh century, and at Kition, provide numerous examples to illustrate this brilliant and sumptuous phase of Cypriot culture.

The Phoenician presence

We have seen how contacts with the Syrian coast increased throughout the Bronze Age and reached a peak during the period that followed. One proof of this is the presence of an Aegeo-Cypriot colony at Ugarit.

In the tenth century the Phoenicians, that is, the Canaanites inhabiting the central portion of the Syrian coast, entered a period of intense activity. Exploiting the situation in the Middle East created by the decline of the great kingdoms following the invasions of the second millennium, they dispatched their ships to conquer the Mediterranean.

The exact time at which they established themselves on Cyprus is a matter of controversy. Certainly, on their voyages to the West they must have made use of the island's ports, with

HEAD OF A MAN.
Cypro-Archaic II (560–540 B.C.).   *Kasaphani.*   *Terra-cotta. Height: 25.5 cm.*
Cyprus Museum, Nicosia.

VOTIVE STATUE.   *Limestone.*
Height : 73 cm.   *Cypro-Archaic (seventh or sixth*
century B.C.).   *Cesnola Collection.*
Metropolitan Museum, New York.

which they were unquestionably familiar, since their fleet carried Cypriot exports intended
for the Oriental market.

However, G. Hill, who has studied the question, concludes that at that distant time the
Phoenicians probably did no more than occupy a few places on the coast, conveniently situated

for trading with other coastal communities and the inhabitants of the interior. It seems likely that they did not push inland until about 550–525 B.C., with the connivance of the Persian conqueror. At any rate, data derived from epigraphic sources and historical information supplied by Menander of Ephesus show that they opened their first trading post at Kition in the eighth century, paying annual tribute to the metropolis. The young Syrian colony was not long in developing, and a century later, on the acropolis of Bamboula, near the ancient port, an imposing temple was built and dedicated to Herakles-Melkard, a great divinity worshipped at Tyre, the "king of the city," who presided over navigation. At this point the question arises: Has there been a Phoenician influence on the art of Cyprus?

Actually, the art of the Phoenicians was itself a product of the many vicissitudes of Phoenician history. It appeared in the second millennium as an amalgam of Egyptian and Aegean borrowings to which Asian and Mycenaean elements were subsequently added.

Thus, in the domain of the arts the role of the Phoenicians was that of intermediaries, a role that went hand in hand with their principal activities, trade and navigation. It is impossible to detect any true synthesis of their art and that of the native Cypriots; on the other hand, it would be wrong to conclude that Cypriot art remained completely unaffected.

Salamis

The excavations on the site (necropolis, P. Dikaios for the D.A.C., 1957; V. Karageorghis starting in 1962; and his successor, J. Pouilloux, and others for L'Institut F. Courby of the University of Lyons, begun in 1964 in the southern sector and still continuing) have not only revealed the urban structure of the city and its architecture but, thanks to the exploration of the necropolis, have also made a notable contribution to the historical patrimony of the island and to our knowledge of contemporary funeral customs.

As we have seen, Salamis claimed to have been founded by Teucer, "the lion-hearted," as he is called in Homer. The first ruler of the city and high priest of Zeus, he is said to have founded the dynasty of the Teucrides after the manner of the Kinyrades of Paphos.

Legends are usually interwoven with historical fact, sufficiently so to constitute evidence of what actually happened, especially when the account is supported by literary sources. This is true in the case of Salamis.

It remains to be shown that myth and epic are consistent with the archeological record, which is still very fragmentary.

The traces of dwellings found near the port above a crag and the shards of proto-white painted ware dispersed in the soil, together with the discovery of a tomb in the maritime quarter – containing a rich find of jewelry and 250 vases – link the site with the first half of the eleventh century. But the silence that envelops the whole of Cypriot archeology for the next three hundred years makes it impossible to reconstruct the history of the city and its life before the end of the eighth and the beginning of the seventh century.

CENTAUR.
Cypro-Archaic (625–500 B.C.).

Ayia Irini.

Terra-cotta. Height: 28 cm, length: 16.5 cm.
Cyprus Museum, Nicosia.

132

FOUR-HORSE CHARIOT.
Cypro-Archaic (625–500 B.C.).　　　*Ayia Irini.*　　　Terra-cotta. Length: 27.5 cm.
Cyprus Museum, Nicosia.

The tombs

The successive changes in living conditions and the prosperity due to a remarkable intensification of economic activity are chiefly reflected in the majestic architecture and the wealth of the tombs.

The necropolis of Salamis is the largest on the island and has the enormous advantage of a continuity preserved over fifteen centuries. What makes it even more important is the presence of large tombs of a very special type.

Intended for kings and aristocrats, they are modeled on the royal tombs of Mycenae, having the same broad trapezoidal dromos sloping gently down to the funeral chamber.

VOTIVE STATUE.
Cypro-Archaic (625–500 B.C.).　　　*Ayia Irini.*　　　Terra-cotta. Height: 46.8 cm.
Cyprus Museum, Nicosia.

In accordance with tradition, horses were sacrificed, a practice mentioned in Homer and common to the Orient and Mycenaean Greece. Skeletons of these animals, in full harness, have been found in several of the monuments. It has also been established that, starting from the seventh century, new burial customs, previously unknown on the island, were introduced, for example, the rite of the "pankarpia."

The wealth of these tombs is considerable and the abundance and variety of the finds (remains of chariots, skeletons of horses, thrones and litters, incised ivory plaques, precious jewels, ceramic and alabaster vases, household goods) give a clear picture of the circumstances of everyday life and of the royal court and its splendor.

The art of the Geometric period

We are poorly acquainted with the artistic path linking the last manifestations of the Bronze Age with the next phase of human evolution, the Age of Iron.

The new situation created on Cyprus by the destruction of the flourishing Mycenaean cities at the hands of the Dorians led to a cultural decline and a falling back on past experience. As life became more stable and the satisfaction of material needs a less pressing concern, the new society was able to reorient itself toward more ambitious goals.

Again, it is through the pottery that this period is best approached. Together with the funerary architecture, it is almost our only source of clues to the progress of the island, historically so obscure. Moreover, the "geometric" element that serves to define the character of the period is most clearly expressed in the decoration of the ceramics.

Origin of the Cypro-Geometric style

There are two principal theories of the origin of the Cypro-Geometric style.

The first maintains that it can be traced to the pottery of the last phase of the Mycenaean (Mycenaean III C 2, end of twelfth-beginning of eleventh century) and to the so-called "granary" style.

The Mycenaean tradition, which can be detected in the sub-Mycenaean and early Cypriot geometric pottery, is supposed to have been reintroduced by the second wave of Achaeans (twelfth century). Following the example of their predecessors, they are thought to have imposed their native art. According to the same theory, it was these Achaeans that colonized Cyprus, and not the Mycenaean merchants of the fourteenth century.

The second theory diverges from the first in maintaining that the sub-Mycenaean, which illustrates a developed phase of the Mycenaean tradition of the fourteenth and thirteenth centuries, was already well established on the island before the fall of Mycenae. Subsequently, it is said to have followed a normal curve of evolution, entering a geometric phase to which the Achaeans are assumed to have contributed.

The lack of data makes it impossible to choose between these two theories with any degree of certitude. There is a tendency to favor the first interpretation, particularly as it is consistent

WARRIOR.
Cypro-Archaic (625–500 B.C.).　　　*Ayia Irini.*　　　*Terra-cotta. Height: 91 cm.*
Cyprus Museum, Nicosia.

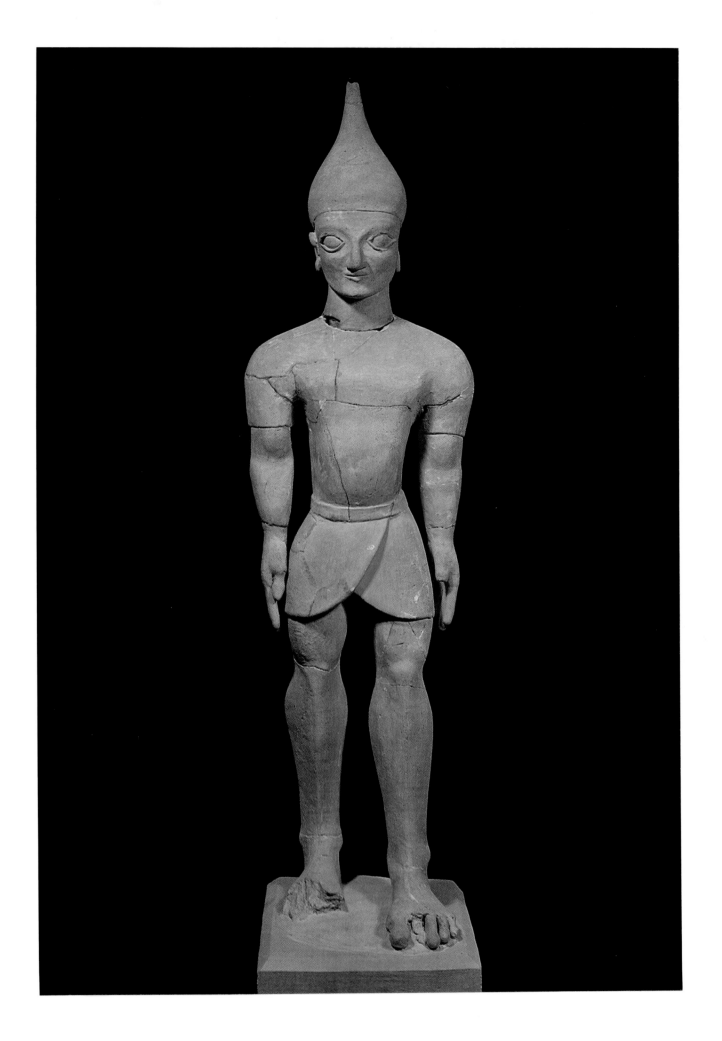

BULL WITH A SERPENT ON ITS BACK.   *Terra-cotta. Length : 36.2 cm.*
Cypro-Archaic (625–500 B.C.).   *Ayia Irini.*   *Cyprus Museum, Nicosia.*

with the results of the exploration of Enkomi. However, the problem of the interruption of
relations with the Mycenaeans at the end of the thirteenth century is worth re-examining (26).

The styles
Before considering the various trends that succeeded one another in the course of this period,
let us first turn our attention to the more permanent characteristics that persisted throughout
the Geometric epoch.

Since ceramics production was so abundant, it has been possible to adopt a classification
based on four categories of decoration.

138

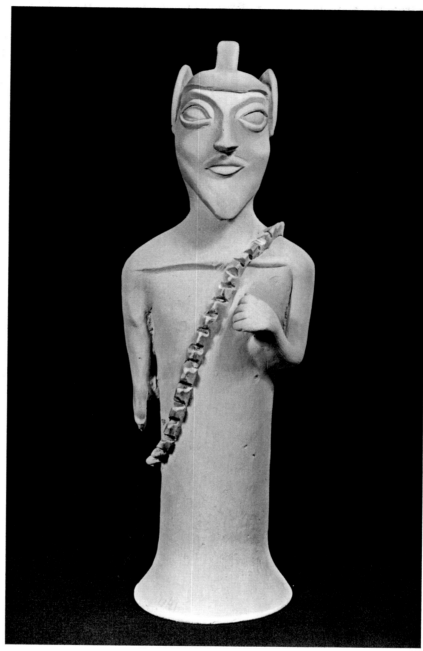

WARRIOR.   *Terra-cotta. Height : 38.6 cm.*
Cypro-Archaic (625–500 B.C.).
Ayia Irini.   *Cyprus Museum, Nicosia.*

In the first, so-called "zonal" style, the body of the vase is divided by horizontal circles into bands usually free of any motif, though to break the monotony the potter does add a certain amount of geometric ornament.

In the eighth century the painter was apparently seeking new solutions. He began to subdivide the horizontal bands into panels. He was thus in a position to "ventilate" his space by leaving voids or to adopt a vertical form of decoration employing simple, and sometimes more elaborate, elements. This more complicated "panel" style permitted considerable freedom in composition and offered the artist opportunities that he had previously been denied.

The style is illustrated by a handsome jar standing on three looped feet (page 98). Probably for ritual reasons, the handles have been given the form of a bull's head. The artist has exploited the oblong shape by dividing it into panels, whose boundaries are indicated by thin vertical lines. The rhythmic movement is accentuated by the geometric motif, whose complex diamond pattern forms both a link and a contrast with the simplicity of the parallel lines.

The "plain-bodied" or "free-field" style is entirely devoid of motifs. Extreme in its simplicity and rigidity, the decoration is confined to circular bands and fillets around the rim, the neck or the base. The free-field style was to reach its apogee in the seventh century, when skilful designers introduced painted motifs. These men succeeded in producing some of the finest works of Cypriot ceramic art.

The last, and rarest, category of decoration is encountered only on lentiform pitchers, whose very shape enabled the potter to develop a vertical sequence of concentric circles that often cover the entire surface of the pot.

All these styles display identical qualities of sharpness and balance, and it is hardly surprising that certain experts should have attempted to compare the severe and rhythmic accent of the decoration with the Homeric hexameter, for this was also the century in which *The Iliad* was probably reduced to its definitive written form.

Principal stylistic features

The progress of each style is a slow ascesis, a painful search for formal affirmation through detours and prolongations. It is well known that the Geometric style of the island was not a local phenomenon. It was a new artistic vision common to the whole Greek world and reflected the spirit of an epoch. It was the fashion of the times, as illustrated, for example, by Attic pottery, which followed the same evolutionary pattern, probably for similar reasons. Did not Mycenae influence both Cypriots and Athenians? What to some extent differentiates the work of the Cypriot artist from that of his Greek brother is the choice of elements.

At first, the Cypriot, still clearly preoccupied with that concern for clarity and balance that Mycenae had bequeathed to Crete, made free use of Mycenaean prototypes, while, at the same time, giving them his particular accent, adapting them to his own tradition, and selecting from the work of his Syrian and Palestinian neighbors whatever best suited his tastes and preferences.

As time passed, growing assurance gave the artisan a measure of his own creative worth. The memory of Mycenae persists in the background, but Cypriot reality can be seen gradually asserting itself.

The use of the wheel, now universal, made it easier to fashion the clay. It also vastly broadened the possible range of forms: bowls and dishes, cups on truncated conical stems and elegant amphoras, ritual vases and votive objects. Admittedly, not everything was original. Certain types are distantly derived from Mycenaean models; others are indebted to

WARRIOR.
Cypro-Archaic (625–500 B.C.).   *Ayia Irini.*   *Terra-cotta. Height: 84.5 cm.*
Cyprus Museum, Nicosia.

WARRIOR.   *Terra-cotta. Height : 58.2 cm.*
Cypro-Archaic (625–500 B.C.).   *Ayia Irini.*   *Cyprus Museum, Nicosia.*

the traditional Cypriot Bronze Age gourd. Occasionally there are rarer forms, such as the horn-shaped vases (page 85) which, according to V. Karageorghis (27), are based on metal prototypes. The elongation of the body with its spiral handle and the simplicity of the decoration contribute to the unusual elegance of this type of pottery.

Other vessels suggest a fusion of both trends and some, though less numerous, recall Assyro-Palestinian ceramics.

The clay is treated with a pale slip over which motifs in dull black or brown or bichrome ornamentation (black and red) of Oriental inspiration is applied.

At first, the decoration is strictly geometric, comprising elements of the Late Mycenaean which, however, have been recast in a severer mold and heavily simplified. Waves, triangles,

CENTAUR.   *Terra-cotta. Height: 31 cm, length: 14 cm.*
Cypro-Archaic (625–500 B.C.).   *Ayia Irini.*   *Cyprus Museum, Nicosia.*

diamonds or squares are concentrated at critical points on the vase, which is generally carefully divided into horizontal zones. Of course, there are also exceptions, cases of the artist trying to avoid the conventions. An example is the handsome amphora on page 81, which is clearly derived from a Late Mycenaean type. At the same time, the body of the vase is elaborately and exuberantly decorated with a variety of motifs that both frame and set off the central composition, in which we once again discern the sacred serpent and the magic bird, themes familiar from the Bronze Age but also from the painted pottery of the Mycenaean III C 1.

At a certain moment, toward the middle of the ninth century, the slow evolution of this phase of the Geometric style ended in a remarkable change. The artist fell under a new discipline leading to personal renewal and revitalization.

The opportunity presented itself in the form of more advanced techniques. One involved the use of a compass fitted with small brushes which the artist spun with a twist of the hand to trace isolated groups of concentric circles. But where formerly one had sensed human warmth, there was now the meticulous discipline, faultless and totally uncapricious, of the machine.

Quick, easy and conventional, and in the long run tiresomely repetitive, this form of decoration was nonetheless to have a glorious career in the course of the Archaic period.

It was a reaction against this austere geometrism that led another school to cover the handsome surfaces of the large amphoras with motifs (birds, stags, ibexes, lotus flowers, etc.) distributed in friezes, or panels in the case of vessels more modest in size, such as bowls and kylikes. Although this innovation certainly demonstrated the need to soften the rigorism of the line, the spirit of the style remained the same, for austerity in art was the discipline of the epoch. Though clearly pursuing realism, the artist insisted on schematizing the drawing which remains subordinate to the composition as a whole.

Human figures, previously so neglected, reappear, especially on the funerary urns which are perfectly adapted, in form and function, to this kind of decoration. Thus, the zone between the handles is ornamented with rich motifs gracefully integrated with the depiction of the scene. A brilliant example is offered by the Hubbard amphora (Nicosia Museum) from the early eighth century. It portrays a burial ceremony in which the dead man is seated on a throne, in the process of drinking through a siphon the contents of a jar, which a servant girl is replenishing. Further off, a sphinx sniffs a flower. The opposite frieze shows women dancing to the tune of a lyre. Such themes are not uncommon either in Greece (Dipylon amphoras) or in the Orient, but the really remarkable feature of the Hubbard amphora is the ritual of drinking through a siphon. According to Xenophon, it was a ceremony practiced in Asia Minor, but it is also illustrated on Syro-Hittite cylinders and a grave stele found at Tel-el-Amarna (28).

The true significance of this important decorative innovation resides in the very stylized conception of the forms. The figures are silhouetted, sometimes reduced to mere threads, no more than a gesture. This cannot be dismissed as lack of skill, since other vases of the same epoch are treated with elaborate realism. It is rather that the ceremony is presented as an ideogram consistent with its spiritual finality and the essential geometrism of the vase.

The ceramics of the period were also decorated in styles other than those already mentioned.

The "free-field" style was very popular, especially for the handsome big-bellied pitchers with a three-lobed mouth and the amphoras. Most of the surface of the vessel was left bare. Only the upper part carried the motif: triangles, circles, rows of chevrons or swastikas, now very much in favor, either filling the zone or isolated against the free field.

The great oval-bellied amphora in the Geneva Museum (page 87) with its elegant handles and color scheme of black, red and yellow gives some idea of the compositional possibilities of simple and traditional motifs. In this case the potter has brought out the austerity of the

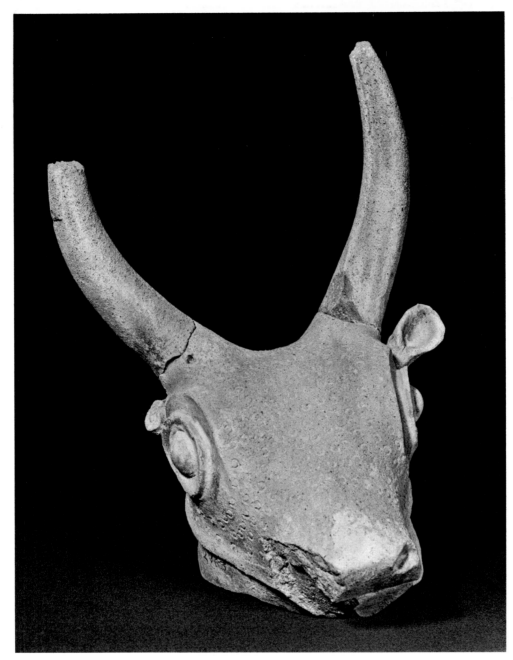

BULL'S HEAD.   *Terra-cotta. Length : 16 cm.*
Cypro-Archaic (615–500 B.C.).   *Ayia Irini.*   *Cyprus Museum, Nicosia.*

composition by keeping the bottom part of the vessel free of all decoration, thus drawing attention to the two ornamented zones confined between broad bands and horizontal concentric circles.

This brief examination of the question of stylistic evolution suggests certain conclusions with a broader bearing.

Thus, the Hellenization of the island, heralded by the arrival of the Mycenaeans, gradually gathered strength in the course of the centuries that followed. This is reflected in the art of

VOTIVE FIGURINE.   *Terra-cotta. Height : 13.5 cm.*

146   *Beginning of Iron Age.*   *Cyprus Museum, Nicosia.*

the potter. The spirit of order and rational inquiry, the tectonic sense of structure, and the taste for narrative, so obvious in the pictorial compositions, are characteristics common to the entire Greek world.

Of course, on Cyprus, with its favored geographical position and affinity for Oriental culture, these traits are somewhat diluted, blended with traditional elements. It is to these multiple influences that Cypriot art owes its antithetical character, at once rebellious and submissive, individualistic and ecumenical, stern and imaginative, qualities whose first fruits are already discernible even in its distant origins.

The minor arts

The tomb offerings are particularly interesting during this period. The chariot tombs discovered at Salamis, including an extraordinary tomb dating from the end of the eighth century, have yielded material of exceptional value because of the rank and importance of the personages involved.

Apart from the chariots themselves, some of their metal accessories may legitimately be regarded as sculpture; for example, there are two bronze axle pins, one ending in a sphinx head surmounted by the head of a warrior. With respect to size (56 cm) it is a find unique in the Middle East. The incrustations in blue *pâte de verre,* the clothing, the breastplate and the helmet, which recall those of Assyria, are so many precious details illustrating the level of technical skill and artistic concern of the craftsman.

Other accessories reveal the same pursuit of luxury and perfection: harness and trappings, rosette pendants, all decorated in a style that has affinities with Assyrian art; bronze supports in the form of stylized flowers ornamenting the yoke of the chariot; iron fire dogs ending in a ship's prow; the decoration of two bronze cauldrons.

According to Karageorghis, who excavated these tombs (29), all these objects may have been the products of Cypriot workshops, but they betray a strong North-Assyrian and chiefly Urartaean influence.

Apart from metal fittings, these same tombs have yielded many ivory reliefs, gold and silver plaques, and jewelry of exceptional quality and delicacy of execution. Two thrones were once covered with finely worked plates of ivory, silver, and blue *pâte de verre.* The remains of a bed, a stool, and a censer, all in solid ivory, attest the wealth and splendor of the Cypriot rulers, who had no cause to envy their Eastern neighbors.

These pieces, probably imported by coastal traders, are in the Phoenician style with Egyptian influences, a style much in vogue in Syria and Palestine during the eighth and seventh centuries.

COLOSSAL STATUE (upper portion).
Cypro-Archaic II (560-540 B.C.).   *Tamassos.*   *Terra-cotta. Height: 82 cm.*
Cyprus Museum, Nicosia.

VOTIVE FIGURINES.
Terra-cotta.
Cypro-Archaic II (beginning of sixth century B.C.).

1. Offering bearer. 2. Offering bearer. 3. Warrior.
From left to right. Height: 14.7 cm, 19 cm, and 15.8 cm.
Cyprus Museum, Nicosia.

THE ARCHAIC PERIOD (700–500 B.C.)

Events on Cyprus

The wars that shook the Middle East at the end of the eighth century did not spare Cyprus.

When the continual clashes that gradually exhausted the warring powers finally ended, the Assyrians were left with the upper hand. Soon they had extended their dominion to the Anatolian coast and landed on Cyprus. Of what happened then history tells us little. We do know from the stele discovered at Kition and the Assyrian archives that the local potentates surrendered to king Sargon II. As for the relations between the suzerain and his subjects, it would seem that, apart from the annual tribute, the protectorate was fairly flexible and a certain amount of internal political autonomy was tolerated.

The Assyrians did not stay long on Cyprus. After a few decades the island was returned, for another century, into the hands of its own monarchs. These years were marked by a notable cultural renaissance to which the Assyrians contributed many Oriental elements.

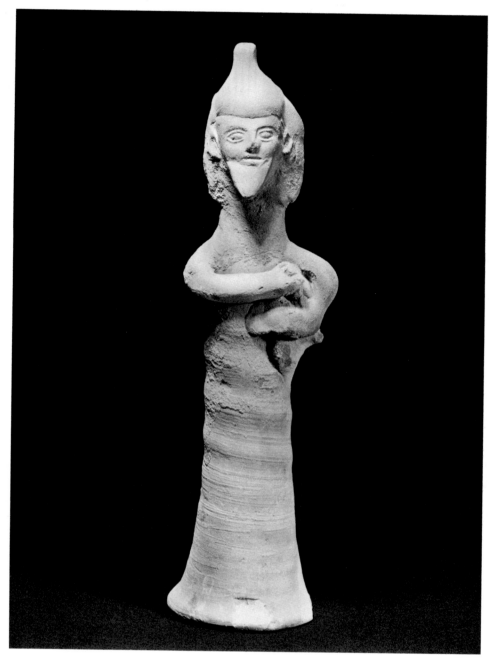

WARRIOR.   *Terra-cotta. Height: 33 cm.*
Cypro-Archaic II (beginning of sixth century B.C.). Cyprus Museum, Nicosia.

The naval battle in which Apries triumphed over the combined fleets of the Cypriots and Phoenicians again tipped the scales in favor of the Egyptians. Herodotus tells us that Amasis, exploiting this victory, became the first Egyptian king of Cyprus. Diodorus of Sicily recalls the Pharaoh's generous offerings to the island's temples. The few documents relating to the occupation are insufficient, however, to give a clear idea of Egyptian policy. But there can be no doubt of the effect of their presence on Cypriot culture and art.

Nonetheless, the inhabitants, despite the weight of the foreign yoke, could not forget their traditional past and their emotional and racial bonds with the Greek world. Contacts with the Aegean multiplied and the barter trade, facilitated by vessels bound for the Greek colony of Naukratis in Egypt which called regularly at Cypriot ports, grew daily in volume. This would also explain the large quantities of Rhodian pottery found at Amathus and on the south coast.

As the skies darkened and the Persian threat loomed, the Cypriots prudently allied themselves with the stronger side, under whose influence their neighbors the Cilicians had already fallen. Cyrus accepted the self-serving cooperation of the islanders and, in return, granted them semiautonomy. Thereafter (525 B.C.) the island formed part of the fifth satrapy, but internal affairs remained the responsibility of the local potentates, whose images continued to appear on the currency.

The Ionian revolt against the Persians 499 B.C. found the Cypriots solidly on the side of the Hellenes despite the defection of the persophile kings of Kition and Amathus, where the opposition of the Phoenician minority prevailed. The heroic intervention of Onesilos, new king of Salamis and champion of the Greek cause, who besieged the two cities, had no effect on the outcome of the war. Despite the destruction of the Phoenician fleet by the Ionians, the treachery of Stasinos, king of Kourion, tipped the scales. Onesilos was taken prisoner and beheaded. Salamis bowed before the might of the conquerors. Gorgos was restored to his throne, and the Persians made the islanders pay dearly for their rebellion. The insurgent leaders were replaced by others better disposed toward the occupiers and when, in 490 B.C., Xerxes was preparing to conquer Greece, the Cypriots sent 150 triremes to fight on his side.

The art of the Archaic period

Ten centuries of foreign occupation with only intervals of autonomy left their mark not only on the social and religious institutions but also on the culture and art of Cyprus.

The presence of the occupiers made itself felt on various levels. Changes in taste were accompanied by an iconographic and technical renewal.

The transition from Geometric to Cypro-Archaic art followed a path parallel and sometimes similar to that followed in Greece. There were, however, certain digressions. A different spirit lies at the source of the inspiration due to the persistence of conservative undercurrents, weakened somewhat by the immediacy of the foreign presence. This period, among the most brilliant of Iron-Age civilization and one of the most original and glorious of Cypriot culture, is distinguished by its Oriental character.

The blossoming of an art endowed with Oriental elements and a quite unusual flexibility is not unconnected with the surrender of the island to the Assyrians and the Phoenician presence, which had grown stronger in the interval.

The geometric rigorism that so pervaded the spirit and the work of the previous epoch has become blurred and muted, though, of course, it has by no means been forgotten. Broad traces of it are preserved in certain types of pottery and in the statuary, which was then beginning to make its appearance.

GRINDING GRAIN.   *Terra-cotta. Length : 10 cm.*
Cypro-Archaic II (600–500 B.C.).   *Tamassos.*   *Cyprus Museum, Nicosia.*

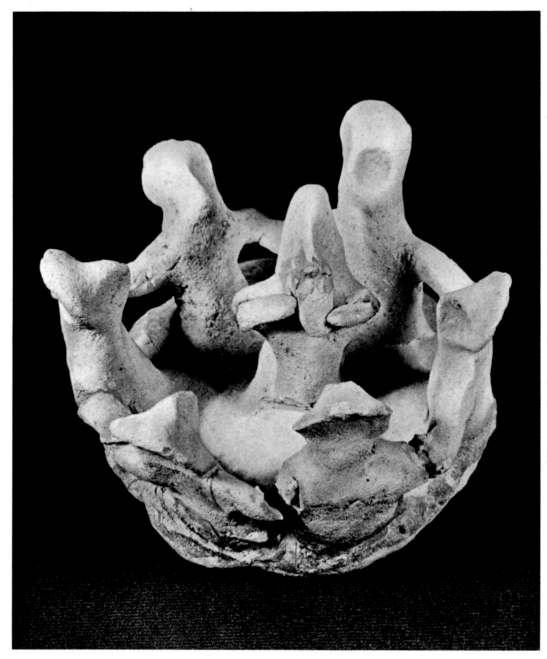

RITUAL DANCE.
Cypro-Archaic II (600–500 B.C.).

Terra-cotta. Diam.: 10 cm.
Cyprus Museum, Nicosia.

The work of the potters

Although sculpture may have played the leading role, responding to the needs of the palace and temple architects, and was at last assuming monumental form, the pottery offers better examples of that slow transformation that led from cold logic to an explosion of the imagination.

The tendency, already apparent at the end of the previous period, to break away from the challenge to nature represented by the severe discipline of geometric art now became more

FEMALE VOTIVE STATUETTE.
Greco-Phoenician period (750–550 B.C.).

Terra-cotta. Height: 23 cm.
Cyprus Museum, Nicosia.

pronounced and developed into a revolt, imposing its own conception and original vision. Not that the conservative tastes of the old rationalists were totally repudiated. Nothing is more difficult than the modification of visual habits, whose slow transformation can be traced through time right up to the present day. Thus, the logic of the ornamentation that characterized the two styles of the preceding period the type with straight horizontal fillets and the concentric circle type continued to be applied (pages 101–105). It even developed, stimulated by original motifs, and drew new life from combinations or fusions of the two designs (page 107).

The three methods of decoration, by zones (page 115) by panels (page 102), and free-field (pages 114, 117, 119, 121, 122, 123, 125, 127), remain the same, their application being determined by the structure of the vase. But the motifs have been enriched by an Oriental admixture.

The styles
The archeologists distinguish the various styles according to regional characteristics.

The Eastern style
This coincided with the Phoenician penetration into areas of the East and South and has a sharp flavor of Anatolian fantasy.

More than ever before, the decorator gave free rein to his imagination, enriching his figurative repertoire from the singular world of winged monsters, griffons, and sphinxes, which were later to find their way into mythology in the form of Pegasus, the winged horse.

Need one add that the borrowings from the East never acquired the terrifying aspect of Oriental mysticism? Their decorative side, so keenly appreciated by the Cypriot, was seasoned with a pinch of humor that rarely extends to the grotesque. The decorative catalogue still includes the entire range of familiar fauna: horned animals symbolizing virility and fecundity (goats, stags, and especially the bull, pages 109, 115, 117, 121, 123), the bird (pages 122, 126, 127), and the fish. These motifs were familiar because they had already been used by the artists of the Mycenaean. However, in view of the six centuries that separated one period from the other, it would be rash to talk of a stylistic renewal. It was more probably a question of the rediscovery of an ancient practice, traces of which had persisted through time (30).

Thanks to its geographical position, Cyprus was able to act as intermediary in the textile trade between the Orient and Greece. This explains the presence of certain Oriental motifs such as the lotus, palmetto, rosette, etc., inspired by fabrics of Syrian or Egyptian origin.

All this ornamentation invaded the panels and virgin surfaces of the panel ware and free-field pottery (pages 121, 122, 123). But the necks of large amphoras were reserved for very elaborate geometric decoration mingled with lotus flowers (page 103) and more rarely human figures.

SCENES OF CHILDBIRTH.   *Terra-cotta. From left to right. Length : 11 cm, and 10.3 cm.*
156   *Cypro-Archaic II (600–500 B.C.).*   *Cyprus Museum, Nicosia.*

COLOSSAL STATUE
OF HERAKLES.
Limestone.   Height: 217,2 cm.
Cypro-Arch. II (about 600 B.C.).
Cesnola Collection.
Metropolitan Museum, New York.

The success of "free-field"
There can be no doubt that in the free-field pictorial style the artistic verve of the Cypriot is
expressed to best advantage. Stimulated by the Oriental example and freed from all constraint,
the painter used the surface of the vessel like a large canvas on which his talents could be

VOTIVE STATUE IN EGYPTIAN COSTUME.   *Limestone. Height: 136.5 cm.*
158   *Cypro-Archaic II (600–500 B.C.).*   *Cesnola Collection.*   *Metropolitan Museum, New York.*

unhesitatingly deployed. The rather lusterless clay was coated with an ivory slip on which quadrupeds, birds, fish and floral motifs (pages 110, 111) were traced with precision, freely or in stylized form. Hunting scenes (pages 119, 121) of Oriental inspiration, already encountered on gold and ivory objects of the Late Bronze Age, were also popular.

One of the motifs that appears to have been held in special esteem is the bird. Its origin remains rather obscure. But as early as the sixteenth century it is to be found on Assyro-Palestinian pottery from the eastern part of the island, which was in direct contact with neighboring Anatolia. Two centuries later, it appears again, though less frequently, on Cypro-Mycenaean pottery, whereas during the Geometric period it seems to have lost its popularity with the public. Yet it majestically adorns the free-field pitchers of the Archaic without a geometric context.

One of the finest examples is offered by a composition on an oval pitcher (page 127) in which the bird is spearing a fish with its long beak. The design, stylized and extremely precise, is enhanced by the very restrained use of black and purple bichromy on a whitish ground. When this vessel is compared with two similar ones (pages 122, 126) the difference in treatment is easily perceived. The first version is distinguished by its elegance, the steadiness and assurance of the artist's hand, the lightness of the composition, which, despite the inclusion of a much greater number of motifs (fish, swastikas, tree, etc.), floats easily in space. As for the other two, the clumsiness of both the contours (page 122) and the geometric detail, the lack of proportion in the distribution of motifs over the surface, and the careless execution identify them as the standardized work of an artisan.

No less worthy of attention are an amphora (page 115) decorated with bulls confronting each other on either side of a stylized lotus flower and a pitcher with a bull amiably sniffing a flower (page 117). Thanks to their seductive charm they deserve a place beside the best Mycenaean treatments of similar themes.

The first of these motifs was probably reintroduced to Cyprus by the conquerors, for in the Orient the "confrontation of bulls before a sacred tree" has a very long religious tradition.

The influence of ivory-carving, the use of incised lines to bring out anatomical detail, is apparent in all this work, where a similar technique is sparingly employed to suggest a third dimension (pages 117, 118, 122, 125, 127, etc.) (31). Metal objects were worked in the same way, for example, the famous bowl of Ras Shamra (32).

This new treatment of the motifs is linked more closely with a decorative compulsion than anything else. It is a pretext adopted by the artist in order to exercise his imagination, a sign of the free expression of ideas and temperament. One has only to glance at the engaging images involving human figures (pages 114, 119, 121, 125). Full of life and humor, they are far removed from any conventional repetitive form. Everything is observed: pose, movement, sometimes an intentionally droll expression (pages 114, 119, 125). Moreover, everything is interpreted (page 121), the fruit of the artist's temperament and his participation in the invented creation. This taste for originality, which we have already noted in the early art of

MALE STATUE.   *Limestone. Height: 177.5 cm.*
Cypro-Archaic II (about 500 B.C.).   *Lefkoniko (Famagusta).*   *Cyprus Museum, Nicosia.*

MALE HEAD.   *Limestone. Height : 45 cm.*
Cypro-Archaic II (600–500 B.C.).   *Musée du Louvre, Paris.*

the Bronze Age, can be vividly sensed in much of the work of this period in which the artist, working within the new social framework, is free to select his prototypes and vary and transpose them as his imagination suggests.

The same spirit, the same trend toward imaginative renewal, is observable in the forms, restrained only by the structure of the vessel, which imposes its own imperatives. Variants of classical models, the barrel shapes have been elongated to permit a better utilization of the

COLOSSAL MALE HEAD.   *Limestone. Height : 60 cm.*

Cypro-Archaic II (about 550–530 B.C.).   *Lefkoniko (Famagusta).*   *Cyprus Museum, Nicosia.*

surface. The pitchers are more voluminous, more swollen, with a dainty little neck and a pinched mouth. Like the rhytons, they are intended to suggest birds. The bowls, in great variety, and the jewel boxes (pyxes) are exquisite. But every crest is followed by a trough. The latter phases of the Eastern style show signs of fatigue. It may be that for commercial reasons production was becoming industrialized. From this point on, the entire vessel is smothered with Oriental motifs (lotuses, rosettes, palmettos), which choke every surface. The artist appears to have been seized by a "horror of the void." The favorite motif is now the "sacred tree," an elaborately drawn and conventionalized lotus plant between two birds or two figures. It should be noted, moreover, that this new attitude is not, strictly speaking, Cypriot, since it is also expressed in the Orientally inspired pottery of the south of Greece and the Peloponnesus.

The Western style

Whereas the pictorial spirit dominated the production of the east, whose potters were more exposed and more amenable to Oriental suggestion, the conservative western artisans, remote from the great international centers, were less receptive to the flow of new ideas. This, at least, is one hypothesis, supported by the nature of the finds.

How much do we really know? The primacy of pure geometric motifs, so conspicuous during the preceding period, is rigorously respected, but it should be added that this time the emphasis is placed on the concentric-circle type of decoration, reinvigorated, however, by a search for new compositions. The techniques vary: broad "vertical" circles traced with brush and compass, between the free spaces small concentric circles (page 105) or groups of concentric circles inscribed in a series of stepped vertical fillets, intersected by another series of fillets girdling the belly of the vase (page 107). Here, too, the variations are innumerable. Using the same elements distributed in various ways, by modulating their thickness, color, and density, it is possible to achieve results that ennoble the form by virtue of their rhythmical relations and decorative charm.

The west also made use of three styles. Free-field was preferred to pitchers decorated with series of concentric circles, vertical or horizontal, a form of ornamentation open to abuse and one that ends in becoming wearisome owing to the superabundance of motifs.

One problem that has preoccupied the specialists is that of the interaction between Greek and Cypriot art. In some cases, for example, the tall-stemmed bichrome krater with bull's-head handles (page 109) and the krater decorated with white meanders on a red ground (page 113), the imitation of Greek geometric motifs is flagrant; in others it is difficult to determine the source of the original decoration. The same applies to the linear ornamentation on a free field described above; yet when one considers that during the Archaic period Greek pottery – and, in particular, that of Rhodes, Crete and the Cyclades – was exposed to Cypriot influences, there is a strong possibility that this design originated on the island.

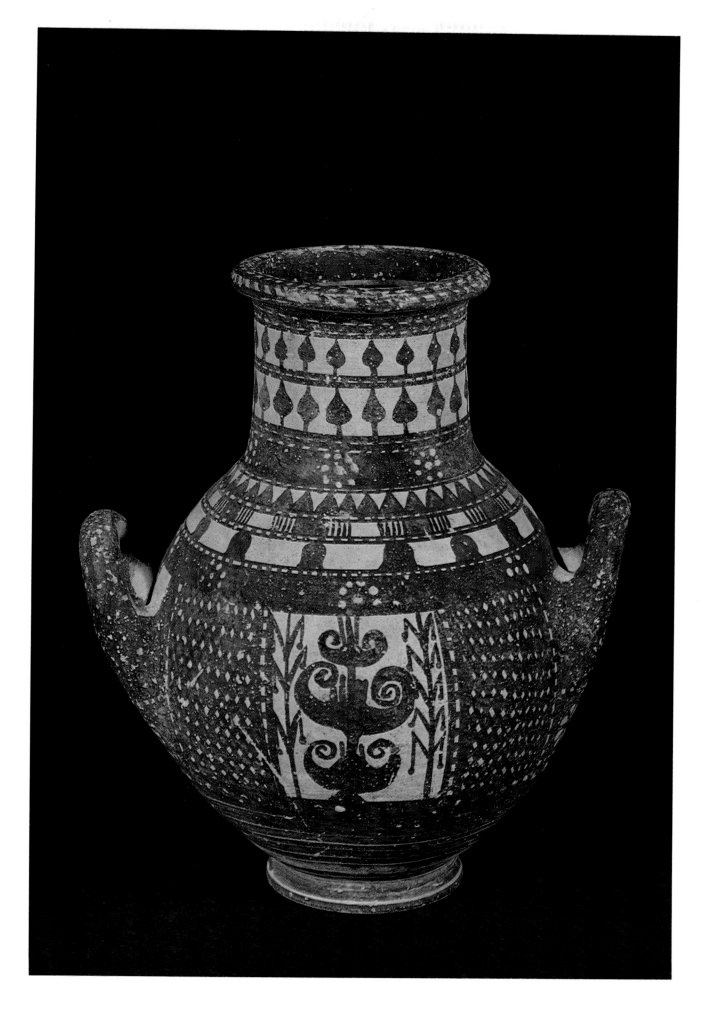

SARCOPHAGUS WITH LID.   Procession. Advance guard and royal chariot. Colored limestone.
Height: 157.5 cm, length: 239.4 cm, width: 109.2 cm.   Cypro-Archaic II (about 600–550 B.C.).
Amathus (Limassol).   Cesnola Collection.   Metropolitan Museum, New York.

Despite their resistance to all forms of modernism, the western potters were not always able to maintain their initial stand. Sometimes, though not often, it is possible to observe a fusion of the two styles as a result of the intrusion of figurative motifs into the abstractions of the ornamental context.

As for the forms, their evolution followed the same courses as in the other competing regions.

Red-colored ware

Together with the white-slip and bichrome ware, which were in full flower toward the end of the Persian occupation, the Iron Age saw the appearance of a red-colored pottery. The decoration is dull black, though as a variant there may be additional motifs in white. Thanks to the color contrast and the broader range of possibilities, the potter often succeeded in creating unusual effects.

The beginnings of this special kind of pottery can be traced to the Geometric period, just before the middle of the ninth century, but it continued to be produced throughout the Iron

PRIEST OR VOTIVE STATUE, HOLDING BIRD AND INCENSE BOX.
Limestone.   Height: 164 cm.
Cypro-Archaic II (before 500 B.C.).   Cesnola Collection.   Metropolitan Museum, New York.

Age in forms similar to those of the white-slip ware. According to E. Gjerstad, this production has been shown to be of Syro-Palestinian origin. The variant, on the other hand, is later, first appearing in the seventh century. Apart from the color, the applied motifs are much the same as those used in the other styles. Thus, they begin as a simplified version of the geometrism of the west. In fact, the combination of black and red tended to make the images heavier, an effect that the more sensitive artists did their best to avoid.

Subsequently, the style also passed through an Oriental phase with the repertoire of motifs with which we are already familiar, all painted in white. Ceramics of this type retained their vitality during the Classical period, when obvious traces of Greek ornamentation with figures in red or black gave the work an uncommon elegance.

Sculptured ceramics

During the Archaic period sculptured ceramics experienced a revival throughout the Greek world, possibly connected with the advent of monumental sculpture and its influence on public taste. However this may be, these vessels failed to excite the same interest in the Cypriots. Of course, there was a long tradition of decoration on the island, but it was a rather specialized tradition. Thus, the anthropomorphic vases of the Cypriots cannot be compared with the production of Samos or Rhodes.

Vases bearing a sculpted female figure, often holding a miniature pitcher, achieved considerably popularity. An example is the pitcher discovered at Polis tis Chrisochous (page 189), where the simplicity of the decoration (bands encircling the body of the vessel and discrete ornamentation of the neck) serves to supplement the modeled form. Here is one of the early signs of that characteristic restraint and austerity in evidence throughout the Classical period.

FROM THE CLASSICAL ERA TO THE ROMAN EPOCH (475-58 B.C.)

The historical context

After the naval battle of Salamis and the collapse of their hopes of conquering Greece the Persians clung even more tightly to Cyprus, and when the Athenians tried to liberate the island in 478 B.C. the fierce resistance of the occupiers compelled them to break off the attack. Although the expedition was a failure, it at least had the effect of making Persian policy more flexible. A second liberation attempt (in 449 B.C.) succeeded in restoring the Greek kings of Marion and Vouni, where the new sovereign Stasioikos remodeled the palace along Greek lines and built the temple of Athene. But the two Persian bastions of Kition and Salamis still held out. Though the Greeks won victory after victory on land and sea, eventually peace came and following the treaty of Kallias (448 B.C.), under which they renounced their claims in the eastern Mediterranean, Cyprus was left to its fate and a new period of Persian oppression began.

PILLAR-STATUE OF A MAN WEARING A CONICAL CAP.

Limestone. Height: 65 cm.   Cypro-Archaic II (about 535-525 B.C.).   Cyprus Museum, Nicosia.

HEAD OF A MAN.
Cypro-Archaic II (about 500 B.C.).

Limestone. Height: 35.2 cm.
Cyprus Museum, Nicosia.

The thirty-seven years of Perso-Phoenician occupation had fatal consequences for the cultural development of the island. After the wars, the cities fell into ruin. Historic Salamis was reduced to a shadow of its former self, whereas Phoenician Kition experienced its time of greatest glory. The Phoenician dynasts behaved even more harshly than their masters. Everything Greek was abhorrent to them, they forbade the inhabitants to practice arts and crafts, and not until the succession of Evagoras I (411 B.C.) were the Cypriots to know better days. The reign of this great philhellenic king was a long series of battles aimed at unifying the

FEMALE VOTIVE STATUE.
Cypro-Archaic II (500–475 B.C.).

Limestone. Height: 61.5 cm.
Private Collection.

island. Finally, exhausted, he was obliged to conclude with the Persians a pact (386 B.C.) that restricted him to Salamis, where he lived in peace until his assassination in 376.

There followed a period of disorder and palace conspiracies that lasted about forty years, ending in the alliance between Alexander the Great and Pnytagoras, who had fought by his side at Tyre.

The incorporation of the island into the Hellenistic empire after Alexander's death in Babylon (323 B.C.) also marked the end of its independence. For a time, the successors of the great Macedonian, too busily engaged in killing each other, left Cyprus alone, and the sovereigns of the isle prudently confined themselves to their own affairs. The calm did not last long. The dissension between Ptolemy and Antigonos soon transformed Cyprus into a vast battlefield. For about thirty years all was destruction and discord. For two and a half centuries after the fall of Salamis in 295 B.C. the island was no more than a Ptolemaic possession. During the reign of Cleopatra the governor of Cyprus took the title of king, though his power was strictly limited. In 58 B.C., under a feeble pretext P. Clodius Pulcher, tribune of the people, caused a law to be passed that turned the island into a Roman province.

The pottery

After the peace of Kallias, Cypriot art entered upon a rapid decline. Except for a few bright moments, it was to lose all its original character and Cypriot civilization was to be identified with that of the Ptolemaic world and later the Eastern Empire.

Social changes and technical innovations that reduced the price of pottery of all kinds brought ceramic ware into disfavor with the public.

Finally, the molded glass technique and the invention of the blowpipe by the Syrians delivered the *coup de grâce*.

In the face of competition from the increasing use of metal vessels, ceramic imitations began to be produced. A typical example is the oval pitcher with a long cylindrical neck and a projecting lip.

Thus it was only natural that there should have been a reduced demand for ceramics as compared with other objects of art better suited to the refined tastes of the wealthy. Apart from glassware, the work of the goldsmiths and carvers also enjoyed the favor of the ruling classes for whom it held many flattering attractions.

Some idea of their preferences can be gained from the bone jewel box (page 201) on which the figure of the god of silence, Harpocrates, has been carved in a lascivious pose.

The sculptured oenochoes, to which we have already referred, were revitalized by diversifying the graceful modeled figurines (pages 185, 189). The usual motif was that of a woman sitting or reclining on top of the vessel and holding a pitcher (pages 185, 189) or a bull's head. But, as in the terra-cotta compositions, another increasingly fashionable motif was the winged god. He and the female figure beside whom he stands probably symbolize Eros and Psyche. Like the winged victory, this motif was copied from Greek models.

MALE HEAD.
Cypro-Archaic II (500–475 B.C.).

Limestone. Height: 31.5 cm.
Cyprus Museum, Nicosia.

CENTAUR AND NYMPH.   Limestone. Height: 18.3 cm, length: 15 cm. Cypro-
Archaic II (600–475 B.C.). Amathus (Limassol). Musée d'Art et d'Histoire, Geneva.

This very special type of vessel, which appears to have been derived from the anthropomorphic pitchers, was very popular during Hellenistic times. Since the form was never
modified, specimens are dated according to the style of the figurines.

The decoration no longer bears any trace of strain or tension. It involves little more than
the application of formulas or the imitation of Greek themes, occasionally with minor
transpositions. The preoccupation with naturalism has become more insistent, which
explains the disappearance of the austere geometrism of concentric circles. The new appeal

BEARDED HEAD WITH LAUREL WREATH.   Limestone. Height: 48.5 cm.
Cypro-Archaic II (500–475 B.C.).   Cyprus Museum, Nicosia.

of nature is expressed in motifs that include birds, stylized leaves, and plants mingled with conventional geometric decoration. The stag's-head rhyton shown on page 195, though of great individual beauty, to some extent sums up these remarks. Its form is derived from bronze or silver vessels of the same type popular with the Achemenides, while its decoration is merely an imitation of the Greek red-figure style.

During the Hellenistic period Greece was the undisputed mistress of the arts.

Henceforth the ceramics were to lack all distinguishing local characteristics, the forms were those of the past, the decoration plain white or lustrous black-and-red.

"Sigillated" ware *(terra sigillata)*, so-called because of the mark or stamp *(sigillum)* used to sign the vase, was the commonest pottery of the Roman period, being used extensively in all the provinces of the Empire. In all probability, it came from the East, where pottery molded in relief was already in use at the end of the fourth century B.C. The best known centers of production were Arretium in Etruria, Candarli near Pergamon, and certain places in the south of Gaul. The decorative relief was obtained by molding the vase. The same term is also applied to wheel-thrown pottery, such as the "plain-glazed."

The mosaics of Paphos

With the expansion of Greek civilization and the adoption of the "city" structure in the eastern kingdoms, autonomy enabled the rulers to satisfy the needs of resurgent religion and the requirements of political and social life. Personal affluence prompted displays of public magnificence.

While the plastic arts were on the decline, architecture became the vehicle of this aggrandizement.

The reconstruction of the Cypriot cities involved the erection of numerous splendid public buildings, royal residences, sanctuaries and temples, the remains of many of which, especially from the Roman period, can still be seen today.

At Salamis, with its glorious past, where every conqueror has left his imprint, the archeologists have already uncovered the gymnasium, the theater, the stadium, and an amphitheater from the second and third centuries A.D. Most of the buildings were decorated with sumptuous mural mosaics and frescoes; marble statues have also been found.

The same is true of Kourion, where the stadium, the theater and the temple of Apollo bear witness to the ancient splendor of the city. The discoveries made in other cities of the island, where the search has not been pressed so hard, are less important, but the presence of stadia, theaters, etc., such as those found at Salamis, Kourion, Nea Paphos and Soloi, is strongly suspected.

One of the most highly prized discoveries of recent years is that of a Roman villa of the third century A.D. whose spacious rooms are entirely paved with mosaics (excavation supervised by K. Nicolaou for S.A.C., 1962. The work continues).

HEAD OF YOUNG MAN WITH LAUREL WREATH.   *Limestone.*
Height: 30 cm.   *(Fifth century B.C.)*   *Cyprus Museum, Nicosia.*

The mosaics are divided into panels depicting hunting scenes or mythological subjects (page 205) with Greek inscriptions giving the names of the figures portrayed. The panels are framed by friezes composed of repeating geometric and floral elements, birds (page 206), and fruits.

The quality of the work demonstrates the level of perfection attained by the mosaicists of that period. Not only were they adepts in their own craft, they were also familar with all the secrets of painting. The foreshortening, the three-dimensional effects achieved by subtile

VOTIVE STATUE OF NAKED MAN.   *Limestone. Height: 53 cm.*
Cypro-Archaic II (510–500 B.C.).   *Cyprus Museum, Nicosia.*

gradations, the balanced and skilful structure, the rendering of movement and facial expression, the general harmony of inspiration, technique and composition combine to give these mosaics, rightly regarded as the finest on the island, their truly exceptional value.

THE ADVENT OF SCULPTURE

As we have seen in skimming through the history of Cypriot art, there is so far no evidence of any sculpture, either statuary or monumental, earlier in date than the beginning of the seventh century.

The only possible exceptions are the bas-relief of a female figure on the walls of a Bronze-Age tomb at Karmi (1800–1600 B.C.) and the bronze gods at Enkomi (twelfth century).

These two cases give pause for reflection, since they suggest the existence of some kind of activity in this direction difficult to document in our present state of knowledge. Considering that the excavators have concentrated their attention almost exclusively on the funerary monuments of those remote periods, it is only natural that they should have unearthed only idols, statuettes, and various small ornaments formed in stone, clay or metal.

Statuary is associated with palaces, temples and public buildings, which presuppose the existence of urban centers. Now, on Cyprus the earliest such monuments date from the Late Bronze Age, the best examples being two temples at Enkomi (twelfth century). The minor sanctuaries of the agricultural communities, of which the terra-cotta model found at Vounous is the oldest trace, were probably too small and unpretentious to have contained religious statues of any size.

All this is no reflection on the Cypriot artist, whose technical ability, skill and keen plastic sense have been clearly in evidence since the very beginning of his civilization, in his unique idols and statuettes, in the figurines and sacred animals that decorate his pottery, and in his terra-cotta models of religious ceremonies and piquant scenes from rural and domestic life.

It is obvious that in spite of occasional clumsiness – not every artist can be a master – the art objects of that distant age are characterized by a taste for realism that ends in the conscious pursuit of extreme stylization and schematization.

Such art, never gratuitous, could not but adapt its expression, form and dimensions to the goals it pursued and the imperatives of creation.

Thus, as soon as circumstances were favorable, monumental statuary bloomed.

The precedents

The island of Cyprus has no marble quarries but abounds in clay and a soft limestone suitable for carving. The plastic artist was quick to take advantage of these natural resources. This is proved by the excavations, but legend, too, acknowledges the importance of working in clay,

BEARDED HEAD WITH LAUREL WREATH.   Limestone. Height: 39 cm, width: 28 cm.
180   *Cypro-Archaic II (600–475 B.C.).*   *Pergamos (Larnaca).*   *Cyprus Museum, Nicosia.*

WREATHED MALE HEAD.
Height : 12.5 cm, width : 9 cm.
Lefkoniko (Famagusta).

Limestone.
Cypro-Classical I (475–400 B.C.).
Cyprus Museum, Nicosia.

attributing the beginnings of the ceramics industry to king Kinyras. There is, however, another reason for the interest in clay, that is, the ease and rapidity with which it can be molded, qualities essential in a material to be used in a system of mass production.

That is why even during the Neolithic and particularly in the Chalcolithic the primitive carver occasionally laid aside his chisels and made his first attempts to mold the local clay.

During the Bronze Age the art of modeling often reached beyond the utilitarian level appropriate to a primitive agricultural society to achieve new forms in which an esthetic concern is apparent. Zoomorphic (pages 25, 34, 49) or ritual (page 29) vessels, plaque idols

LYRE PLAYER.
Cypro-Classical I (475–400 B.C.).

Terra-cotta. Height: 19 cm.
Cyprus Museum, Nicosia.

(page 33, 53) and strange fertility figures (pages 58, 69) form a whole repertoire in strong contrast with the work of the preceding period. The discovery of metal in the third millennium does not seem to have deflected attention away from the traditional techniques.

Eighteen centuries were to pass before the use of the lost-wax method was proposed as an alternative to clay or stone, and it is significant that this was preceded by the development of overseas trade.

Was this delay due to ignorance of metal-beating and smelting? However this may be, from that moment on there is no lack of evidence of the Cypriot's natural aptitude and affection for the plastic arts. First of all, there are the sacred animals, the bull of Katydata still influenced by the form of the rhyton; then the man seated on a throne (page 78), now in the Louvre, a lively caricature which, according to Schaeffer, combines Syrian and Egyptian influences, and the young horned god (page 77) and patron of mines found at Enkomi, of which the former, in particular, is equal in treatment and technique to the best work of much later periods.

Appearance of monumental sculpture

This high point was followed by three centuries of obscurity. The archeological record is generally blank, but particularly so in the case of sculpture. Nothing has been found that might throw light on the process of gradual transition, the period of constant trial and error that must have preceded the appearance of stone and terra-cotta monumental sculpture as technically advanced as that of the seventh century. Indeed, by that time the level of skill was so high that it was possible to fire life-size and even larger statues (Colossus of Tamassos, page 149). Only the Etruscans were to achieve an equal mastery of the art.

Although the long Cypriot tradition probably contributed heavily to the evolution of monumental sculpture on the island, local aspirations could never have been brought so quickly to fruition without initiation into the methods and techniques of the advanced civilizations on the mainland. These contacts with Oriental neighbors and their presence on Cyprus starting in the seventh century must certainly have played a preponderant role in the transmission of knowledge and ideas.

The relation between style and material

Every art depends on its means of expression. This is particularly true of sculpture, which presents numerous problems not encountered in other disciplines. The materials, tools and working methods constitute many traps that the sculptor must avoid if he is to breathe life into the inert mass without betraying his original idea.

Often the material dictates the form. The unsure hand first seeks a soft and docile medium, like clay, wood or limestone, which are easily tamed. Marble, basalt and granite, nobler and less yielding, demand a greater mastery.

Cyprus lacks hard materials. There are only alluvial clays at the base of the mountains and soft friable limestones readily dissolved by moisture. This explains the rigid and monumental style peculiar to the island, since the work can only be carved in a solid block or pillar, without irregularities or protuberances. Gesturing legs and arms are carved separately and then attached to the body.

The Cypriot artist successfully adapted his methods to these unavoidable technical limitations. He worked in the flat, rarely piercing through the block, profiting from the broad surfaces of the chest and back. Fear of breaking the stone made him cautious. He joined the legs and made the arms hang close against the body. If one of them had to be bent, he turned

PITCHER WITH SCULPTED FEMALE FIGURE. Terra-cotta. Height: 39 cm, width: 12 cm.
Cypro-Classical I (475–400 B.C.).   *Cyprus Museum, Nicosia.*

RELIEF REPRESENTING TWO LIONS ATTACKING A BULL.
Bronze.   Length: 23.5 cm.
Cypro-Classical I (475–400 B.C.).   Temple of Athene-Palace of Vouni.   Cyprus Museum, Nicosia.

it at right angles across the chest. The modeling of the face was based on the same principles, low relief that never develops into opposing masses (pages 130, 131).

Thus, Cypriot statuary is ruled by restrictive principles that dictate its style. The law of frontality, common to all forms of primitive sculpture, produces statues frozen into a rigid pose, inanimate, insensitive to the movement that engages the body in a communion with life, that expresses an action or a thought. Not that such movement is always explicit, for there is a "mobile immobility" in which the tense dynamism is only suggested. The "contained" power of an archaic sculpture, the simplified detail, the stylization that readily turns to rhythm, all these plastic qualities, usually neglected by the savants, appeal much more strongly to our modern taste than all the technical perfection of the so-called Classical era.

Despite these constraints, working within these narrow bounds, the artists made the most of such freedom as they were allowed. They used engraved decoration and, above all, they exploited the opaque and delicate grain of the limestone to apply color, a procedure that

ANTHROPOID SARCOPHAGUS.   Marble. Length: 211.5 cm.
Cypro-Classical II (400–350 B.C.).   Kition.   Cesnola Collection.   Metropolitan Museum, New York.

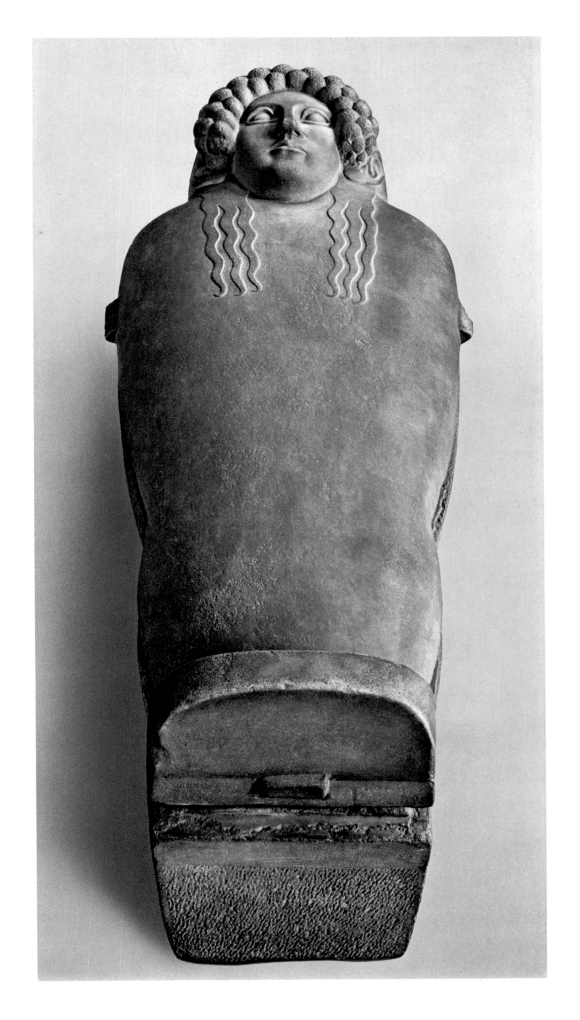

enabled them to suggest relief and sensitize the bright light to the beauty of the form. The eyes and hair are picked out with sky blues or bright reds, the latter also being applied to the clothing, accessories and a thousand ornamental details. Yellow, on the other hand, is used only to suggest the metallic brilliance of jewelry.

Taking full advantage of the limited chromatic possibilities, the artist set out to flatter and give new life to the stone. What an astonishing spectacle, this motley crowd of worshippers, servants, priests, and sacred animals, all motionless for eternity. The brilliant polychromy, shattering the stern silence of the temple, imposes its majestic presence on the dazzled vision of the faithful, in an eternal questioning of their destiny.

The types

During the Classical and Archaic periods the local gods, now identified with the Greek pantheon, continued in favor. The cults of Aphrodite and Apollo reached their culmination. Their universality is attested by the temples found throughout the island. Grouped around them were the lesser gods, new arrivals from Phoenicia, Anatolia or Egypt, brought to Cyprus by the capricious currents of history.

To judge from the excavations, votive figures were the commonest form of Cypriot sculpture. They were erected within the precincts of the sanctuaries or covered temples, around the altar at which the god was worshipped.

The sculptors were very active and their repertory of figures appears, at first glance, to have been quite extensive. On closer inspection, the variety is seen to have been confined to certain traditional models, handed down from one generation to another.

The architect, like the sculptor, worked essentially for the divinity. The distance between gods and men was never very great. The gods intervened in human affairs, as described by the bards and poets. Thus, on Cyprus the statuary was conceived as an ex-voto, an image expressing the desire of the believer to enter into intimate communion with and reside under the eternal protection of the god. The numerous terra-cottas now in our possession eloquently attest to these aspirations. The devotee placed himself in the hands of the god, performed ritual acts acknowledging his power and the favorable results of his intervention. He honored him by joining with the rest of the faithful in songs of praise and sacred dances (page 154). He contributed to the material support of the god incarnate by making offerings, fruits and cakes, wine and incense, and sacrificed doves or young animals (pages 150, 151). But these were only transitory acts of propitiation, permanent protection required a continuous presence. His effigy, his double, left in the temple, could represent him and function in his place, guarding against the withdrawal of divine favor.

This religious concept resulted in the large-scale production of certain types of figures standardized in accordance with conventional rules and bearing no trace of individualization. There are "worshippers," pillar statues in stone or terra-cotta, in many different sizes, their arms by their sides or raised in a gesture of adoration, bearing offerings (pages 150, 151);

PITCHER WITH SCULPTED FEMALE FIGURE. Terra-cotta. Bichrome redware. H.: 20 cm.
188   *Cypro-Classical I (475–400 B.C.).   Polis tis Khrysokhou (Paphos).   Cyprus Museum, Nicosia.*

FEMALE HEAD WITH KALAHTOS.   *Limestone. Height : 70.2 cm.*
Cypro-Classical I (475–400 B.C.).   *Cyprus Museum, Nicosia.*

there are "warriors," motionless, abstracted, conscious of the perils that awaited them in that period of continuous strife (pages 141, 142, 145). Other themes, portrayed on various scales, were the dance (page 154), the banquet, and musicians playing the lyre (page 183), flute or drum.

The effigies of rulers and priests are distinguishable only by their particular attributes. Another special type, which first appeared in the fifth century, is the "young acolyte," who must have belonged to a certain class of children consecrated to the cult. Figures of this kind have frequently been found in the sanctuaries at Vouni, Tamassos, Idalion and elsewhere. Other statues wear oriental costume, a reminder of the importance of foreign influences.

FEMALE HEAD WITH KALATHOS.   *Terra-cotta. H.: 27.2 cm.*
Cypro-Classical I (end of fifth century B.C.).   *Cyprus Museum, Nicosia.*

The evolution of ideas during the Classical, Hellenistic and Roman eras took its tone from the international spirit of the times. Cypriot sculpture, having lost all its individuality, descended into provincialism and decadence.

The evolution of styles

The first to make a systematic study of Cypriot sculpture was Sir John Myres, in connection with the publication of the catalogue of the Cesnola Collection (33). His early work has since been modified and supplemented by the findings of the Swedish Expedition following its discovery of the sanctuary of Ayia Irini (excavations of the S.C.E., 1929) (34). This famous

191

site yielded almost 2,000 terra-cotta figurines of all sizes which had been placed around the altar: worshippers, warriors, chariots (page 134), bulls (pages 138, 146), centaurs (pages 133, 143), officiating priests, and two or three pieces in limestone. This abundant material has made it possible to reconstruct the evolution of sculpture on Cyprus since the beginning of the seventh century. Thus, there were evidently three different phases of stone sculpture and seven others of terra-cotta.

Inevitably, the history of Cypriot sculpture also reflects the changing political and military fortunes of the island, the various foreign influences and encroaching civilizations with which it came in contact. Certainly, Egypt played an important role. At a time when relations were close and the Greek colony of Naukratis was in full development it is not unlikely that Cypriot artists found their way to the Nile delta. Egyptian statuary was carved on an imposing scale in hard stone; in the sixth century its stiff, hieratic type of image, softened to conform with the Hellenic vision of man, was to become the Apollo-Kouros.

It is in its oldest phase (625–560 B.C.) that the terra-cotta sculpture retains a certain individuality, though some of the details of treatment and dress betray Anatolian or North-Syrian influence.

The earliest piece of stone sculpture, the upper half of a female figure bearing a bull in her arms as an offering, was found at Arsos. It dates from the first half of the sixth century. The tranquillity of the features, unfortunately disfigured, the flatness and austerity of the modeling, similar to that of the terra-cottas of Ayia Irini, the subtle suggestion of the forms of the body beneath the light draperies, give an idea of what the genuinely Cypriot style of that period may have been like. The "votive statue of a man wearing a Cypriot belt" (page 130), frozen in his unchanging pose, displays a more advanced technique, though the received conventions are still scrupulously respected.

Stylistic similarities can be detected in the famous Colossus of Tamassos (page 149), an exceptionally large (about 10 feet) and distinctively treated piece. The same qualities reappear in the "head of a bearded man" from Kasaphani (page 129) with its sharply delineated features, fixed imperturbable expression, almond eyes, delicately incised eyebrows and stylized beard.

The reign of Amasis marked a turning point for Cyprus. The ability of the Cypriots to assimilate foreign influences is well displayed in their adaptation of Egyptian elements to the local taste. This process gave birth to a mixed style, all severity, but with the Pharaonic impassivity relieved by the supple modeling that illumines the face. It is only in the decorative details of the hair or in the adoption of the costume of the occupier that one can detect the Egyptian ascendancy (page 159). The "Herakles brandishing a club" (page 158) and the "votive statue in Egyptian dress" (page 159) are two eloquent examples of this local language, vigorous and adaptable to a vision that is not without its own instinctive originality. Moreover, Egyptian art never had the same attraction for the local artists as that of the Assyrians. That is why, starting from the middle of the sixth century, it was easily displaced by the

COW.   *Bronze. Length: 19 cm.*
Cypro-Classical I (about 450 B.C.).   Temple of Athene-Palace of Vouni.   Cyprus Museum, Nicosia.

FUNERARY STATUETTE.
Cypro-Classical II (fourth century B.C.).

Terra-cotta. Height: 39 cm.
Cyprus Museum, Nicosia.

triumphant thrust of Ionian civilization. In those days Persia was extending its dominion to both Cyprus and a dozen Hellenic cities on the Anatolian coast, and the highly developed life of the spirit was producing the finest fruits of philosophy. Relations, already long-standing, became even closer under the benevolent eye of the common occupier. Soon the Ionian smile invaded the island, even the centers occupied by the less receptive Phoenicians (Kition). The fusion of inborn and acquired characters is evident in the style whose beginnings are illustrated by the finds of Ayia Irini.

RHYTON IN THE FORM OF A HORNED ANIMAL.
Cypro-Classical II (fourth century B.C.).

Terra-cotta. Height: 19 cm.
Cyprus Museum, Nicosia.

After about 525 B.C. it was to be further strengthened by elements introduced from Greece, particularly the schools of Attica and Aegina.

Thus, the dawn of the fifth century heralded the most brilliant period in the history of Cypro-Ionian art, a blend of grace and moderation, equally attuned to the mind and the body (pages 173, 174, 175). One is welcomed by a thousand tight-lipped smiles, gracious but reserved (pages 161, 162, 171, 179), openly cordial (pages 167, 175, 181), invitingly coquettish (page 177), or even with that element of mockery traceable in the joy of the centaur lightly caressing his nymph (page 174).

Admittedly, the gain in quality is balanced by a loss of originality. There is nothing to distinguish the Cypro-Ionian from the prevailing style in other parts of the Greek world, except perhaps its greater robustness and candor, qualities of provincial artists less prone to finickiness than the masters of the metropolitan centers. Limestone, moreover, does not lend itself readily to overrefinement. This is reflected in the technique. The draperies, which generally follow the conventional teaching of the prototypes (pages 161), occasionally (page 167) achieve a sharpness and decisiveness that approach the ideal.

The gestures and attitudes (pages 171, 179) suggest a certain awkwardness, as do the attempts at facial expression. Generally, however, and therein resides his strength, the Cypriot sculptor, with his accumulated experience and the instincts of a craftsman of old peasant stock, does not hesitate to ignore the rules in order to give his art a less idealistic and more realistic accent and forms in which life is more powerfully evoked.

The exhilarating mood of these few decades was dissipated by an unfortunate sequence of historical events. After the Ionian revolt and its aftermath of conflict, Cyprus, abandoned by the Greeks, sank into slavery. Having failed to profit from the brief period (460–449 B.C.) of contact with Attica, whose influence is only occasionally discernible, deprived of their chief source of inspiration and stimulation, the islanders withdrew unto themselves. The result was an increasing inertia and decadence, evidenced by a conventional and wearisome repetition of the same types, revived and treated in a pedestrian, weak and industrialized form (pages 182, 183). And this at a time when the sculptural art of Greece was passing through one of its most glorious phases.

Things improved toward the end of the century with the ascension of king Evagoras I to the throne of Salamis. A fervent philhellene, the new sovereign became the champion of Athenian culture. The last ten years of his life were devoted to the development of trade and the embellishment of the city. Under these conditions artistic production resumed at an accelerated tempo. But the results of this increased activity are lacking in quality, though there were, of course, certain happy exceptions. It has even been claimed, (35), based on a few unusually impressive heads from the sanctuaries of Arsos and Potamia, that a very creditable school of sculpture existed on Cyprus at this time.

Generally speaking, however, all eyes were fixed on Skopas and Praxiteles, but there was little relation between aspirations and performance. As often happens in these cases, the

HEAD OF ZEUS AMMON.
Bronze. Eyes incrusted with silver. Height: 5 cm.
Hellenistic period. Soloi. Cyprus Museum, Nicosia.

HEAD OF OLD MAN.
Terra-cotta.   *Height: 17 cm.*
Hellenistic period I (end of fourth century B.C.).
Pyre of tomb 77, Salamis. Cyprus Museum, Nicosia.

tiarsts tried to recover lost time by making an effort of "modernization," without considering the special circumstances that make a particular movement blossom in a particular place or the chain of logic that leads to a specific result. The phenomenon is not unknown in our own day, when art is often disfigured by the mimicry of the apogones. This was the case on Cyprus, where most of the sculptors became ensnared in a mannerism imitative of the work of the pupils of the great Athenian masters.

The liberation of the island by Alexander the Great in 333 B.C. opened up new perspectives for Cypriot sculpture. The attention of the artists was now drawn to the extraordinary blossoming of the arts in the new capitals of Antioch and Alexandria. But the transfusion came too late to save the patient. Efforts to follow the fashion of the moment inspired by Egypt or Pergamon led only to failure. The entire third century was nothing but a succession of more or less clumsy imitations of Egyptian works of art. In very few instances is it possible to sense the presence of Rhodes, Athens or Asia Minor.

STATUETTE OF A MAN PLAYING THE DOUBLE FLUTE.
Terra-cotta.   *Height: 14.2 cm.*
Roman epoch (third century A.D.).   *New Paphos, house of Dionysos.*   *Cyprus Museum, Nicosia.*

The construction of important monuments, palaces, gymnasia, stadia, forums and theaters created a demand for new kinds of sculpture. The votive statues represented gods, Apollo, Artemis and Demeter being especially revered. The trend in taste was toward a naturalistic realism, and portraiture, which was to become popular after the arrival of the Romans, made a timid appearance. The "philosopher" type, and other models imported from Greece, were typical of the Hellenistic period. Limestone versions discovered at Vouni and Lefkoniko provide examples. The copy, however, is not exact. The type remains the same, but the head has been changed in an attempt to reproduce the features of the Ptolemaic sovereigns or Cypriot potentates, as proved by comparison with medals bearing their effigies.

The beginning of the second century saw a new initiative. The latest art from Egypt, a hybrid style with obvious Hellenistic overtones, was greeted with revulsion. Distaste for the imported product led to the revival of a local style, which persisted into the Roman era. This was the artists' last attempt at "protest." Henceforth they were doomed by an inexorable fate either to accept the art of the Empire or die.

The terra-cottas

Terra-cotta sculpture has its roots in the earliest antiquity. From the Neolithic to the Bronze Age and on into the Geometric period the figures had always been small in size, but the discovery of the sanctuary at Ayia Irini also revealed an important advance in firing and molding techniques that was henceforth to permit the execution of works on a larger scale, more appropriate to the needs of the times.

The pieces that have been unearthed have all the familiar characteristics of the period: an hieratic severity or even harshness, a frozen expression. There are two principal types. The first consists of tubular figures wearing a long chiton, replicas of the pillar statue (pages 139, 145, 150, 151). In some of the larger figures the feet peep out beneath the hem of the robe (pages 141, 169) in a manner reminiscent of certain of the limestone carvings (page 131). By contrast, statues of the second type have limbs detached from the body (page 137). Paint is sometimes used to pick out details of the figure or draperies.

At the other end of the spectrum one finds the statuettes intended for the mass commercial market, the general public of limited means. These depict everyday occupations, such as grinding grain (page 153) and other domestic tasks or scenes from family life. Childbirth, an event of capital importance, is represented in all its crudity and with scrupulous attention to technical detail (page 157). Other more daring themes are rendered in the same spirit. These vignettes, so full of animation and poignancy, cover the whole panorama of human activity. They are an inexhaustible source of information, a visual record of contemporary manners and customs expressed in a popular and spontaneous form.

The free-standing figures are either tubular or shaped from a solid block, decorated in the so-called "snowman" style, primitive and unsophisticated in treatment, but full of spon-

PYXIS. *Relief representing Harpocrates, god of silence. Bone. Height: 11.3 cm.*
Roman period I (first century A.D.). *Kato Paphos, house of Dionysos.* *Cyprus Museum, Nicosia.*

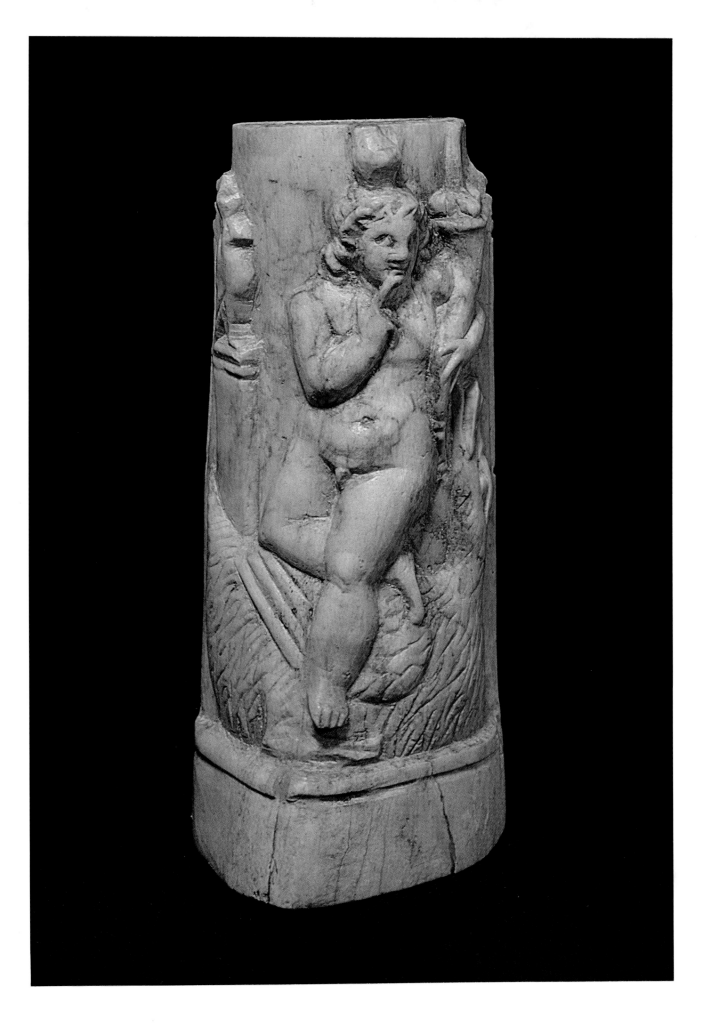

MASK: BEARDED MAN, forehead and hair missing.   Terra-cotta. Height: 16.3 cm, width: 15 cm. Roman period I (first century A.D.).   Kato Paphos, house of Dionysos.   Cyprus Museum, Nicosia.

MASK: NEGRO HEAD.   Terra-cotta. Height: 18 cm, width: 21 cm. Roman period I (first century A.D.).   Kato Paphos, house of Dionysos.   Cyprus Museum, Nicosia.

taneity and charm (page 106). Again there is a variety of types: warriors bearing shields, worshippers with raised hands, musicians, etc. The craftsman is free to play, with irony and humor, on the expressions worn by his homunculi.

Toward the end of the seventh century the mold was introduced, probably from Syria. It was first used to fashion the torso and the limbs, which were then reattached to the body, but in the course of time the process was extended to complete effigies, the details being modeled by hand or picked out in red or black paint.

The Classical period is best illustrated by the material recovered from the sanctuary of Mersinaki and the palace of Vouni, which supplements the finds at Ayia Irini.

My stylistic remarks concerning the statuary apply equally to this minor art, which followed the same prevailing currents in an attempt to satisfy the preferences of the public to which it was addressed.

The working methods were adapted to the market. The molds were now imported from Greece or copied from Greek models. That is why the style is more uniform and closer to the Hellenic spirit than that of the limestone sculpture.

DRUNKEN OLD WOMAN.   *After Myron. Limestone. Height : 14.5 cm.*
Roman epoch.   *Cyprus Museum, Nicosia.*

An example of this technique is offered by the unusual head of a woman wearing a "kalathos" in the form of a tower (page 191). Her imposing aspect and serenity of expression, together with the perfection of the workmanship, recall the splendid Greek sculptures of the period.

A funerary statuette (page 194) representing the dead woman meditating on her harsh fate may be compared with the Attic steles of the fourth century, which depict the same theme and bear the same stylistic traits. Here, the head has been cast in a mold, whereas the body is the work of some Cypriot craftsman.

The finds at the sanctuary of Mersinaki prove that large cast terra-cottas continued to be produced throughout the Hellenistic period. The manual retouching of the cast is a sign of the artist's desire for realism in the portrayal of character.

The repertory of cast figures is much the same as that of the preceding period, though it has been enriched by the addition of various personages interpreted according to local taste. The preferred figures are those of Eros, god of love, who was very popular at the time in all the Mediterranean lands, and the goddess Aphrodite, whose images recall the famous statues of the great masters. The theater provided the inspiration for figures of actors, depicted with great freedom, much humor and ironic zest (page 199), small molded masks, sharp reflections of a fleeting emotion (page 202), and others retouched by hand to represent comedians. It should be noted that the production of masks representing chthonian deities or the presumed image of the believer goes back to the Archaic period.

Grotesque figures appeared, based on various prototypes drawn from the work of the great masters. An example is the statuette of a drunken woman (page 203) after the famous statue by Myron, who worked at Smyrna.

Another, very different aspect of the Hellenistic art of Cyprus has recently been revealed as a result of the excavation by V. Karageorghis (S.A.C., 1965, 1966) of the cenotaph of Nicocreon, the last king of Salamis (36). This monument, the only one of its kind on the island, comprises an exedra and a pyre around which life-size statues were arranged on posts. Modeled in unfired clay, the fragments that have been found, heads of men and women (pages 197, 198) and assorted limbs, show evidence of a very advanced technique and a vigorous realism. The very careful handling of the features and the treatment of the hair recall the art of Lysippus. Karageorghis suggests that the cenotaph may have been erected in honor of the royal family, which perished in tragic circumstances in 311 B.C.

Metalwork

So far we have been concerned only with the sculptural output in materials peculiar to the island, limestone and clay, which determined both the character of the statuary and the Cypriot style.

At the same time, however, the metal industry was developing along parallel lines. Its products were expensive and therefore designed to appeal to a more refined and more exacting public.

In general, the progression of styles was the same as for the sculpture in stone and clay, with certain minor variations.

Metal-working is a versatile art capable of producing objects that range from domestic utensils, weapons, and various accessories, either figurative or merely ornamental, to the delicate creations of the jeweller and statues large and small.

The search for such objects has been well rewarded. Palaces, sanctuaries and tombs have been prolific, even generous. This was the case with the palace of Vouni, where the Swedish Expedition had the exceptional good fortune to discover the royal treasure, a store of silver

TRIUMPH OF DIONYSOS.   Detail: old man leading a pair of panthers drawing the chariot of Dionysos.   Mosaic pavement.   Roman period III (third century A.D.).   Roman villa, Paphos.

205

FOLIATED SCROLL WITH BIRDS.   *Detail of border around a grape-harvesting scene.*
Mosaic pavement.   *Roman period III (third century A.D.).*   *Roman villa, Paphos.*

coins and precious jewels hidden in a moment of panic at the time of the fire that destroyed the building in 380 B.C.

The temple of Athene at Vouni yielded a number of valuable pieces of Greek origin, such as a bronze relief (page 186), a true piece of goldsmith's work, representing two lions devouring a bull. This was an Oriental motif adopted by the Greeks and appears to have been linked with the worship of the goddess. The splendid solid-bronze cow (page 193) from the same site, now in the Nicosia Museum, is probably an imitation of a famous work by Myron.

The sarcophagi

The Cesnola Collection in the Metropolitan Museum includes several fine sarcophagi.

As we have seen, in the distant past coffins were not used, the dead being laid directly in the earth.

The earliest examples of sarcophagi bear an obvious resemblance to wooden coffins. Others reflect the influence of the decorated terra-cotta work of Clazomenae. After the fifth century the stone sarcophagus became rather rare. A fine limestone specimen, richly decorated with bas reliefs and accented here and there with color, has been found at Amathus. One of its panels represents the solemn progress of the royal cortege (page 166).

HEAD OF BEARDED MAN.   *Limestone. Height : 31.5 cm.*
(400–500 A.D.). Temple of Zeus Lavranon (Fassoulas).   *Cyprus Museum, Nicosia.*

At the end of the fifth century Hellenized versions of the Egyptian mummy (page 187) were being imported from Egypt.

In conclusion

The history of Cypriot art does not end, of course, with the Roman period. But the great diversity of influences which follows – from the hegemony of the Eastern Empire with its Byzantine art to the Turkish occupation and, in passing, the Frankish and Venetian phases – induces us to stop our survey here. The message of beauty bequeathed us by the ancient Cypriot world has, in spite of the richness and variety of its works, a certain unity; and the perception of objects in totally different spirits would only disturb it.

COMPARATIVE TABLES (periods, culture, excavations, finds, etc.)

Epochs on Cyprus	Dates	Greece	Middle East – Orient	Events on Cyprus	Religion and culture
Neolithic IA	6500 5800–5250	*Mesolithic*	Mural paintings of *Catal höyük* Houses and place of worship *Hacilar* (5500). Clay statuettes of the Mother Goddess.		
IB	5250–4950	*Neolithic* (5000). Undecorated, then incised pottery. Figurines, idols.	*Anatolia:* monochrome redware. *Mesopotamia:* figurines of the Mother Goddess. *Iarmo:* figurines.		
IIA	4950–3500 3500–3200	*Pre-Sesklo.*	Troy I.		
IIB	3200–3000	*Early Sesklo.*		Colonization by Eteocypriots, probably from Anatolia.	
		Late Sesklo.			
Chalcolithic I	3000–2500	*Chalcolithic* (2600).	Troy II (2600). Local dynasties at Sumer.	Discovery and exploitation of copper mines (third millennium). Colonists arrive from Anatolia and Syria.	Erimi culture. Probable introduction of cult of the Fertility Goddess.
II	2500–2300			Cyprus becomes a place of call on the Aegean route.	Burial rites similar to Aryans.
		Primitive Hellenic I–II–III.		Expansion of trade (pottery, copper, wood) with Syria and Egypt.	
Early Bronze or *Early Cypriot* IA	2300–2200		Troy III (2200).	Arrival of foreign civilization on Cyprus, probably from Anatolia. Peaceful infiltration.	Probable introduction of bronze technology from Anatolia.
IB	2200–2100 2100–2000			Stock-raising and farming. Exploitation of copper mines.	Development of trading relations with Crete, the Aegean, Syria, Assyria and Egypt.
II	2000–1900	*Bronze* (2000).	Hittites appear in Anatolia.		
III	1900–1800	*Middle Hellenic* I–II–III.			
Middle Bronze or *Middle Cypriot*	1800–1600		Crete at its apogee. Mari prospers (eighteenth century). Antagonism between the Hyksos and Egypt. Ca. 1775. Foundation of Hittite kingdom.	The Hyksos (end seventeenth century).	Growing prosperity. Export trade with the Middle East.
Late Bronze or *Late Cypriot* IA	1600–1450	*Late Hellenic* I 1660–1550 (Mycenaean)	Great migrations in Europe and Asia.	Pharaonic domination of Cyprus (toward middle of second millennium)	
IB	1450–1400		Egyptians predominant in the East.		
IIA	1400–1300	II fourteenth century Mycenaean IIIA Expansion of Mycenaean trade III		Mycenaeans arrive and drive the Eteocypriots into the isolated parts of the island.	Introduction of Mycenaean worship and customs, syllabic writing. Diffusion of Arcadian.

Principal excavations	Sites	Finds	Sculpture	Architecture
DAC, 1936–1939 and 1946. SCE, 1927 and 1931.	Khirokitia Petra tou Limniti.	Objects in stone and obsidian. Pottery (towards end of period).	Andesite idols.	Dwellings of the "tholos" type. Tombs.
	Troulli.	Objects in flint and obsidian, stone bowls. Lustrous red and red-on-white ware.		
Pennsylvania University Museum and DAC, 1947 and 1950.	Sotira. Kalavassos.	Necklaces – Combed ware.	Idols in stone and steatite.	Dwellings hollowed out of the rock, oval or rectangular with rounded corners.
Cyprus Museum, 1933–1935.	Erimi and other sites.	Stone and flint utensils, first occurrence of copper utensils, red-on-white ware.	Steatite idols.	Dwellings similar to Kalavassos. Round dwellings.
DAC, 1942.	Ambelikou (Soli).	Lustrous redware, red-and-black ware, bowls in the latter, pitchers.		
DAC, 1943.	Philia. Kyra, Khrysiliou, Ayia Paraskevi, Vasilia, etc.	Adoption of oriental forms. Continuation of local forms, bowls and pitchers in lustrous red or red-on-white ware.		Tombs of mixed type.
Cyprus Museum, 1931–1932. BSA, 1937.	Vounous.	Local pottery much influenced by oriental ceramics. Exuberance of decorative motifs.	Plaque idols (Brett-idols) – lustrous redware. Incised decoration.	Cemeteries.
DAC, 1942. DAC, 1943.	Ambelikou. Kalavassos, Margi.	Complete fusion of oriental motifs. Cypriots try to impress own character. Great variety of forms. Lustrous red ware. Ornament in relief.	Model of temple from Vounous.	Dwellings with several rectangular chambers. Rock-cut tombs with dromos.
J.L. Myres, 1894.	Kalopsidha, Karmi, Krini, Ayios Sozomenos, Nitovlika, Paléos, Koutela.	Personification of vases. White-slip ware. Black-slip or red-on-black ware. Objects, tools and weapons in bronze.	Karmi relief. Plaque idols. White-painted ware. Incised decoration.	House at Kalopsidha. Fortresses. Cemeteries, complex tombs related to those of Syria and Palestine.
British mission, 1896. SCE, 1927–1930. Schaeffer, 1934–1968. SAC, 1948–1956.	Enkomi.	White-slip ware. Ring base ware.		Richest necropolis of the Late Bronze. City.
	Enkomi. Kition.	Mycenaean pottery in large quantities. Motifs of the Mycenaean repertory. Exuberant style. Gold jewelry. Diadems, rings, earrings, etc. Ivories. The Kition rhyton.		

SCE – Swedish Cyprus Expedition.

COMPARATIVE TABLES (periods, culture, excavations, finds, etc.) *continued*

Epochs on Cyprus	Dates	Greece	Middle East – Orient	Events on Cyprus	Religion and culture
II B *Late Bronze*	1300–1230	Thirteenth century. Mycenaean IIIB.		Important events at Enkomi. Building of a new city.	
IIIA	1230–1190	1250–1200 Sub-Mycenaean. End thirteenth century. Mycenaean IIIC1.		Achaean colonization following the Trojan War (ca. 1200). Foundation of Salamis and other cities by the Achaeans.	
IIIB	1190–1150		The Sea Peoples.	Invasion of the Sea Peoples.	
IIIC	1150–1050			Destruction of the Late Bronze Age cities by an earthquake.	The poet Stasinos composes "Songs of Cyprus."
Cypro-Geometric I	1050–950	*Protogeometric* 1100–1050 1000–900 *Geometric* 1000–900–750		1000–707. Cyprus independent. Nine city-kingdoms governed by hereditary kings. Tenth century. Phoenician infiltration. Colonization of Kition and Amathus.	Discovery and exploitation of iron. Fertility goddess Hellenized and becomes Aphrodite. Adoption of usages and customs of the Greeks.
II	950–850			Ninth and eighth centuries. Obscure period.	
III	850–700	*Oriental* 750–600	Turmoil in the Middle East.	742–707. Cypriot thalassocracy.	Great prosperity (tenth-eighth centuries).
Cypro-Archaic I	700–600	*Archaic*		707. Assyrian domination. Phoenician penetration.	New burial customs (eighth century).
II	600–475	Black-figure vases (500).	612. Fall of Nineveh. 499. Ionian revolt against the Persians.	569–546. Egyptian domination. 546–411. Persian domination. 499–498. Revolt of Onesilos.	Amasis adorns the temples with numerous offerings.
Cypro-Classical I	475–400	*Classical* Red-figure vases (400).		*Persian influence* 480. Cypriots join Xerxes in his expedition against the Greeks. 450–499. Kimon's expedition to Cyprus. 448. Treaty of Kallias. 448–411. Perso-Phoenician occupation. 411–386. Evagoras I, king of Salamis.	Arts and crafts in decadence. Great prosperity of Salamis.
II	400–325		333. Victory of Alexander the Great at Issos.	332–323. Occupation of Cyprus by Alexander the Great.	
Hellenistic I	325–150	*Hellenistic*	Struggle between Ptolemy and Antigonos.	*Egyptian influence* 298 B.C. – 58 A.D. Ptolemaic period. 295. Salamis falls to Ptolemy.	Deification of Egyptian kings. Peace and prosperity.
II	150–50				Reputation of Cypriot poets and philosophers becomes pan-Hellenic (Sophathos, Dionysos, poets; Eudemos, philosopher; Aristos, historian; Zenon, founder of Stoicism).
Roman I	50 B.C.– 150 A.D.			51 A.D. Cicero proconsul on Cyprus. 58 A.D. Cyprus a Roman province. 79 A.D. Earthquake. Destruction of Hellenistic cities.	
II	150–250 A.D.			332 and 342 A.D. Earthquakes. Cities devastated.	
III	after 250 A.D.				

Abbreviations: BSA – British School of Athens. ¦ CM – Cyprus Museum.   DAC – Department of Antiquities of Cyprus.   SAC – Service of Antiquities of Cyprus.

Principal excavations	Sites	Finds	Sculpture	Architecture
	Mythou, Pygades.			Stone town house.
Schaeffer and DAC, 1946–1958.	Enkomi.	Bronze objects. Ivories.	Horned god (early twelfth century), patron of mines.	Cyclopean walls. Imposing buildings. Temples. Cemeteries. Mycenaean-type tombs.
		Style inspired by oriental tapestries and fabrics.		
	Kaloriziki.	Scepter of Kaloriziki (1050). Rude pottery.		
Necropolis. SAC, 1957–1968. Institut F. Courby of the University of Lyons, 1964–1968 (south sector).	Salamis.	Zonal style. Panel style. Free-field style. Geometric decoration.		
Archaeological hiatus on the island.				
	Cellarka.	Reintroduction of pictorial motifs. Oriental influences.		Chariot tombs of the Mycenaean type.
	Salamis.	Kition stele. Phoenician ivories in the Egyptian style. Objects in gold, copper and bronze.		
		Eastern style. Western style.	Appearance of monumental sculpture (seventh century). Colossus of Tamassos (terra-cotta). Use of the mold (end of seventh century).	
SCE, 1919.	Ayia Irini. Meniko.	White-slip ware. Red-slip ware. Sculptured ceramics.	Two thousand terra-cotta sculptures and figurines found at Ayia Irini. Ca. 550 First stone sculpture (Arsos). Ionian influence. Fifth century. Cypro-Ionian art.	Rustic sanctuary.
SCE	Mersinaki.			
SCE	Vouni.	Treasure of Vouni. Molded glass. Alabasters. Metal vessels. Metal vessels copied in clay.	Decadent sculpture.	Palace of Vouni. Temple of Athene (Vouni). Theater of Soloi. Embellishment of the cities.
		Oenochoes with sculptured decoration.	Influence of Antioch and Alexandria. Realistic heads.	
SAC, 1965–1966.	Salamis.	White-slip ware or red-and-black ornamentation on a lustrous ground.	Cenotaph of Nicocreon (311). Clay statues.	Erection of temples in honor of the kings of Egypt (temples of Osiris and Serapis).
Pennsylvania University Museum, 1934 and 1952. SAC.	Kourion.			Theater, baths and stadium of Kourion. Tombs of Nilaphos. Construction of Arsinoi.
		Sigillated ware.		Construction of road network, aqueducts, forums, gymnasia, libraries, theaters, public baths.
SAC. Continuing.	Paphos.	Third-century Roman villa with finest mosaics on the island.		Beautification of Paphos and Salamis. Reconstruction of the Temple of Aphrodite at Paphos which becomes a famous pilgrim center.

SCE – Swedish Cyprus Expedition.

NOTES

1. *E.O. James,* La religion préhistorique. Payot, Paris, 1959, p. 166 ff.
2. Excavations of the Cyprus Museum, 1931–1932, cf. *P. Dikaios,* Les cultes préhistoriques dans l'île de Chypre. Syria v. XIII, 1932, p. 344 ff. *P.D.* I, pp. 22–24.
3. Excavations conducted by P. Dikaios in 1948 for the DAC and the French Expedition. Cf. *P. Dikaios,* The Bronze Statue of a Horned God from Enkomi, Archäologischer Anzeiger, 1942, *P.D.* I, 41. *V.K.* I, p. 148.
4. *Cl.F.A. Schaeffer,* Götter der Nord und Inselvolke in Cypern, Archiv für Orientforschung, XXI, 1965, p. 59. *V.K.* I, pp. 148–149.
5. Cf. *V.K.* I, pp. 166–169. BCH, v. 91, 1967, pp. 328–348, and *V. Karageorghis,* Excavations at Salamis 1964–1966 (in Greek), RDAC, 1966.
6. *V.K.* II, p. 4.
7. Discovered by the Swedish Expedition in 1929. Cf. *E. Sjöquist,* Die Kulturgeschichte eines Cyprischen Temenos, Archiv für Religionswissenschaft, 1933, p. 308 ff. *P.D.* I, pp. 85–86. *V.K.* I, pp. 200–201.
8. *G. Gl.,* pp. 285–286.
9. *E.O. J.,* p. 137.
10. *G. Gl.,* p. 292.
11. *A. De Ridder* and *W. Déonna,* L'art en Grèce, A. Michel, Paris, 1924, p. 71.
12. *P. Dikaios,* Khirokitia. Oxford University Press, 1953.
13. *H.W. Catling,* Cyprus in the Neolithic and Bronze Age Periods. V. I, p. 7 of The Cambridge Ancient History.
14. *S.C.E.* Vol. IV (I A), p. 106 ff. and *ibid., Sotira.* Philadelphia, 1961.
15. *H.W. Catling,* Cyprus in the Neolithic and Bronze Age Periods. V. I, p. 43 ff. of The Cambridge Ancient History. *P. Aström,* The Middle Cypriote Bronze Age. Lund, 1957.
16. *M.I. Maximova,* Les vases plastiques dans l'antiquité. Paris, 1927. *A. Pieridou,* Anthropomorphic Vases of Cyprus. RDAC, Nicosia, 1968 (in Greek).
17. For the history and decipherment of this writing see *O. Masson,* Les inscriptions chypriotes syllabiques. Etudes Chypriotes, I. Paris, 1961. *Ino Nicolaou,* Le développement de l'écriture chypriote, Bulletin de la Société des Sciences et Lettres. Famagusta, 1967.
18. A propos the problem of the workshops see *H.W. Catling,* in the Annual of the British School of Athens 60, 1955, p. 212 ff. *V. Karageorghis,* Nouveaux documents pour l'Etude du Bronze Récent à Chypre. Etudes Chypriotes, III. Paris, 1965, p. 201 ff., and *idem,* Mycenaean Art from Cyprus. Nicosia, 1969, p. 2.
19. *V. Karageorghis* has been able to identify the authors of several vases found both on Cyprus and elsewhere, see *V. Karageorghis,* A Mycenaean painter of swallows, Archäologischer Anzeiger, Heft 2, 1967; *idem,* Mycenaean Art from Cyprus, p. 4.
20. *Idem,* Nouveaux documents pour l'Etude du Bronze Récent à Chypre. Paris, 1965, p. 201 ff.
21. *Idem,* An early XIth century B.C. tomb from Palaepaphos, RDAC, 1967, p. 1.
22. Since the available data on this period are generally limited, it is only possible to offer tentative dates. Those who have studied the problem (*ibid.,* p. 23, and *V.R. Desborough,* The Last Mycenaeans and Their Successors. Oxford, 1964, 24 f.) are inclined to place the tomb between 1100 and 1050 B.C.
23. *Ibid.,* p. 6.
24. *Ibid.,* p. 6.
25. *A. Leroi-Gourhan,* Origine et diffusion de la connaissance scientifique. Paris, S.E.T., 1953, p. 200.
26. *P.D.* I, pp. 54–55.
27. *V. Karageorghis,* An early XIth century B.C. Tomb from Palaepaphos, RDAC, 1967, p. 21 and Pl. III, 21.
28. *P.D.* I, pp. 77–78. *V.K.* II, p. 17 and Pl. XXI.
29. *V. Karageorghis,* Chronique des fouilles et découvertes archéologiques à Chypre en 1966, BCH, vol. 91, 1967, pp. 337–348.
30. *V. Karageorghis,* Some Cypriot painters of bulls in the archaic period. Extract from "Jahrbuch der Deutschen Archäologischen Instituts," vol. 80, p. 1, Berlin, 1965.
31. *Ibid.,* pp. 10–11.
32. *Ibid.,* p. 12. *C. Schaeffer,* Ugaritica II, pl. 8.
33. His contribution is summarized in two of his books. See *J.M.H.* and *J.L. Myres* and *Ohnefalsch-Richter,* A catalogue of the Cyprus Museum. Oxford, 1899.
34. Cf. *S.C.E.* II, 642 ff.
35. *P.D.* I, p. 94.
36. *V.K.* I, p. 203 ff.

ABBREVIATIONS

P.D.I   *P. Dikaios,* A guide to the Cyprus Museum, Nicosia, 1961.

S.C.E.   *E. Gjestad-Others,* The Swedish Cyprus Expedition. Vol. I–IV, Stockholm, 1934–1938.

G.G.I   *G. Glotz,* La civilisation égéenne. Renaissance du Livre, Paris, 1923.

E.O.J.   *E.O. James,* Mythes et rites dans le Proche-Orient ancien. Payot, Paris, 1960.

V.K.I   *Vassos Karageorghis,* Chypre. Les Editions Nagel, Geneva, 1968.

V.K.II   *Vassos Karageorghis,* Treasures in the Cyprus Museum, DAC, Nicosia, 1962.

J.M.H.   *John L. Myres,* Handbook of the Cesnola Collection of Antiquities of Cyprus. Metropolitan Museum of Art, New York, 1914.

PERIODICALS

BCH   Bulletin de Correspondance Hellénique.

RDAC   Report of the Department of Antiquities of Cyprus.

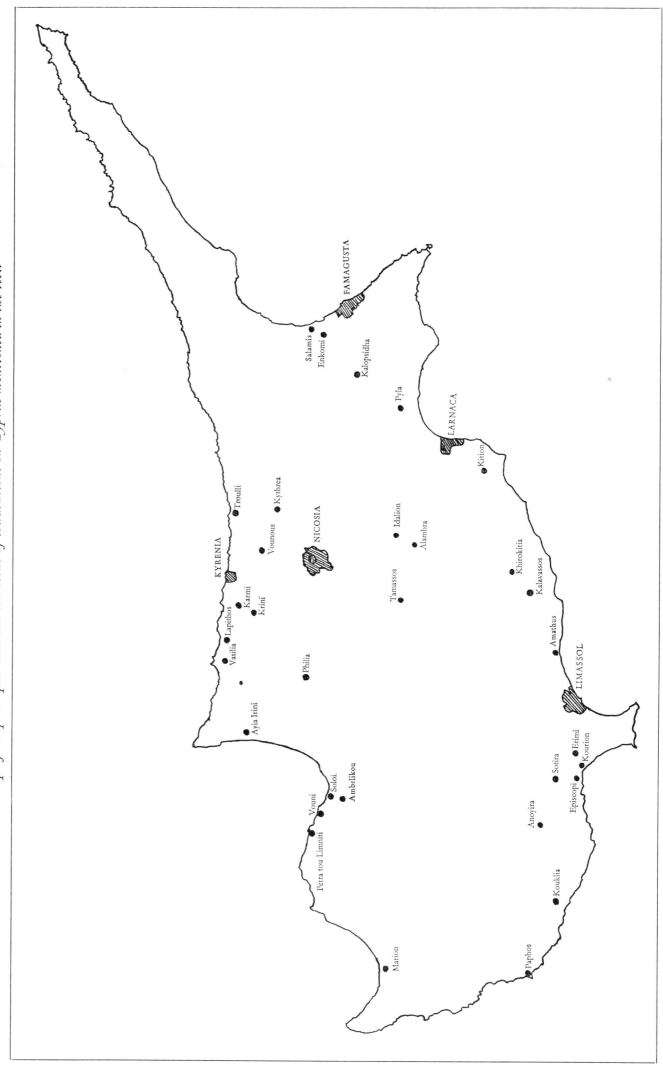

Map of the principal sites and locations of excavations on Cyprus mentioned in the text

SELECTED BIBLIOGRAPHY

The list that follows is confined to a small number of works of general interest not mentioned in the text.

G. Conteneau, *Manuel d'archéologie orientale*. 4 vol. Paris, 1927–1947.

L. Delaporte, *Les peuples de l'Orient méditerranéen*. Paris, 1948.

A. Emilianides, *Histoire de Chypre*. Paris, 1963.

A. Furumark, *The Mycenaean Pottery, Analysis and Classification*. Stockholm, 1941.

G. F. Hill, *A History of Cyprus*. Cambridge, 1940.

V. Karageorghis, *Corpus Vasorum Antiquorum, Cyprus,* I (1963), II (1965). Nicosia.

V. Karageorghis, *Excavations in the Necropolis of Salamis*. Nicosia, 1967.

V. Karageorghis, *Mycenaean Art from Cyprus*. Nicosia, 1968.

V. Karageorghis, *Sculptures from Salamis,* I. Nicosia, 1963.

V. Karageorghis and C. C. Vermeule, *Sculptures from Salamis,* II. Nicosia, 1966.

G. Lafforgue, *La haute antiquité*. Paris, 1969.

K. Nicolaou, *Ancient Monuments of Cyprus*. Nicosia, 1968.

M. Sacopoulou, *Chypre d'aujourd'hui*. Paris, 1966.

Cl. F. A. Schaeffer, *Missions en Chypre, 1932–1935,* Paris, 1936.

K. Spyridakis, *Cypriot Kings of the Fourth Century B.C.* (in Greek). Nicosia, 1963.

Catalogue of the exhibition *Trésors de Chypre*. Paris, 1967. Munich, Milan, Geneva, Belgrade, 1968.

Annual Report of the Curator of Antiquities, Nicosia, 1914–1916.

Annual Report of the Director of Antiquities, Nicosia, 1949–1967.

Journal of Hellenic Studies (from 1949 to 1955 includes a report on the *Archaeology of Cyprus*; from 1956 the same report in *Archaeological Reports*). Published by the Hellenic Society and the British School of Athens.

Printed in Switzerland